Fast-Fold Hexie
QUILTING

A Quick & Easy Technique for Hexagon Quilting

Mary M. Hogan

Landauer Publishing

Fast-Fold Hexie Quilting

Landauer Publishing (*www.landauerpub.com*) is an imprint of Fox Chapel Publishing Company, Inc.

Copyright © 2021 by Mary M. Hogan and Fox Chapel Publishing Company, Inc. 903 Square Street, Mount Joy, PA 17552.

Project Team
Editor: Stephanie White
Copy Editor: Amy Deputato
Designer: Wendy Reynolds
Photographers: Mary M. Hogan (step-by-step photography and pages 7, 9, 19, 23, 26–27, 94–100); New Africa/Shutterstock (page 8); elena09/Shutterstock (page 9); Al Robinson/Shutterstock (page 9); kkmek/Shutterstock (page 17); Monticello/Shutterstock (page 21); Mike Milhalo Photography (jacket and all other photography)

ISBN: 978-1-947163-40-9

Library of Congress Control Number: 2020943611

We are always looking for talented authors. To submit an idea, please send a brief inquiry to acquisitions@foxchapelpublishing.com.

Printed in Singapore

21 20 19 18 2 4 6 8 10 9 7 5 3 1

Dedication

For Rita, Christine, Judy, Carol, Kathy, and Maureen, and the many other women who have helped or inspired me, I dedicate this book to you. Having you in my life has meant so much.

Acknowledgments

Thanks to Landauer Publishing; they took a chance on me and accepted my first proposal. Special thanks to Jeri Simon, Sue Voegtlin, and Catherine Dreiss at Landauer, from whom I learned a great deal about putting together a book. Thanks also to the staff and customers at The Quilting Season in Saline, Michigan, who have created a continually evolving quilting community that I am privileged to be part of.

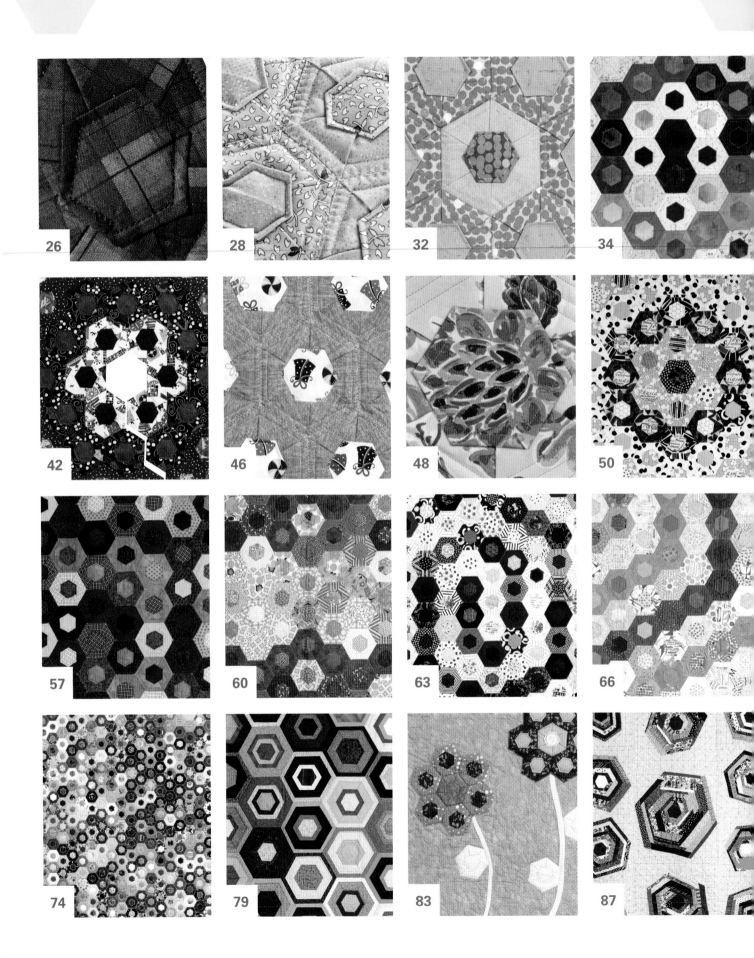

26

28

32

34

42

46

48

50

57

60

63

66

74

79

83

87

Contents

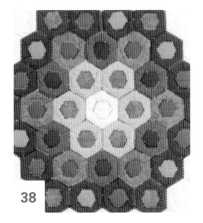

38

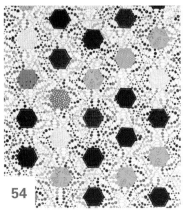

54

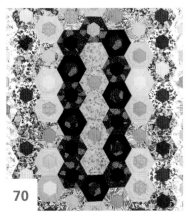

70

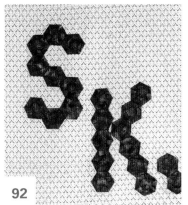

92

Introduction

Fast-Fold Hexies: An Easy, Quilt-As-You-Go Technique

The hexagon shape has long been used in quilting, and many intricate quilts have been designed and made with hexagons. Most hexagon quilts rely on English paper-piecing (EPP), a technique in which fabric is basted to paper hexagon shapes, and the fabric hexagons are then whipstitched together from the wrong side. I love the handwork involved in this technique: cutting out the paper pieces, cutting small pieces of fabric, basting, and sewing hexagons together. With EPP, after sewing the quilt top together, there are still time-consuming steps to complete before you have a finished quilt: remove the paper, make a quilt sandwich with backing and batting, do the actual quilting, and finally add the binding.

The Fast-Fold Hexie (abbreviated throughout the book as FFH) method allows you to make hexagon quilts by hand or machine using a

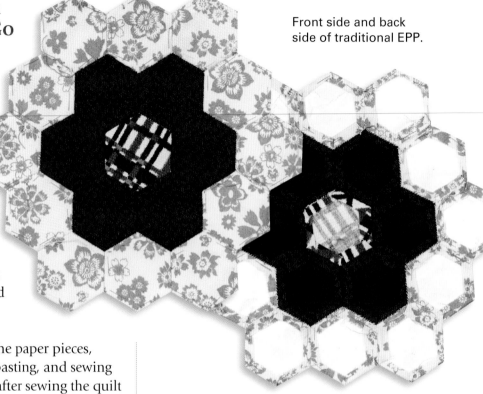

Front side and back side of traditional EPP.

quilt-as-you go technique: start with a circle of fabric, fold it to a hexagon shape, insert batting, add a small folded hexagon topper, and sew. You now have an enclosed quilted hexagon unit with a finished edge, which can be easily sewn to other units. Once the hexie units are sewn together, the project is complete. There is no need to prepare a backing, baste, quilt, or add binding.

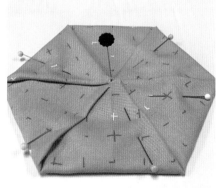

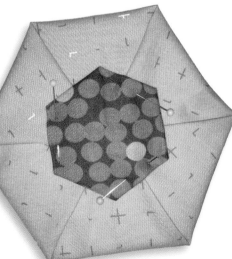

A FFH is made of a base (left) and topper (middle).

Bachelor-button flowers were the original inspiration for FFHs.

I developed the techniques in this book after purchasing *The Art of Elegant Hand Embroidery, Embellishment, and Appliqué* by Janice Vaine. As I made some of the bachelor-button flowers featured in the book, it dawned on me that I was essentially making little hexagons. Over the next few months, and with much trial and error, I worked out how to adapt the folding technique from the bachelor buttons to make hexagon units for quilts. In this book, you'll learn the technique plus get instructions for projects that use fast-fold hexies.

One of the things I love about the FFH technique is that it's portable: you don't have to spend all your time at the cutting table and sewing machine. For example, you can use scissors to cut the circles and batting, then fold and pin the hexies in your lap (I like to place my cardboard work surface on a cookie sheet when folding). You can do all the sewing by hand, or with a sewing machine, or a combination of both. This technique is versatile, and I hope you'll love it as much as I do.

Materials and Supplies

You don't need any special quilting supplies to make these projects, but I do have some recommendations to make the process easier.

✳ **Fabric:** In general, I recommend using high-quality quilting cotton for these projects. This fabric is easier to work with and ensures good results. You can also experiment with flannel fabrics: the texture is fun to work with, but is not recommended for small FFHs (5" [12.7cm] circle hexie bases or smaller), because it is too bulky. Avoid batik fabrics at first: the tight weave is harder to pin and especially difficult to sew by hand. Busy prints may not show up well. Instead try using small prints, solids, and fabrics that read as solids.

✳ **Batting:** I recommend Warm & White® or Warm & Natural® from The Warm® Company for FFHs. This batting is not stretchy and holds its shape better than other batting. In general, I prefer cotton batting, but if you prefer polyester, I recommend Soft & Bright®, also from the Warm Company. This polyester batting holds its shape well and is lighter weight than cotton, which may be an advantage in these quilts. If using other batting, test to make sure you are satisfied with it before cutting hundreds of hexagon batting pieces.

✳ **Thread:** For the most part, I'm not particular about thread and use what I have, which is typically 100 percent cotton, poly/cotton, and polyester. I do enjoy working with 80wt Wonderfil polyester thread, especially for hand sewing. If you use a neutral shade, the stitches nearly disappear, and the thread holds well.

✳ **Needles:** For hand sewing, I don't have specific needle recommendations; I find a needle that works easily with the fabric and thread I am using. When machine sewing, look for a larger needle than what you would use for regular piecing, such as a universal size 90/14 or 100/16. For sewing stacked FFHs (e.g., Homage to the Hexagon, page 79), or if the universal needle does not work, try a jeans/denim needle, in size 90/14 or 100/16. This technique requires you to sew through multiple layers, so a larger needle may be needed.

✳ **Template Material:** You need paper or plastic to make the templates for cutting fabric and batting. For circles that are 10" (25.4cm) or less, I prefer to use full-circle templates and template plastic. For larger circles, I use paper quarter-circle templates. Batting templates require something sturdy, such as plastic or cardstock.

An empty fabric bolt makes a great work surface. You can usually get one for free from your local fabric store.

* **Marking Tools:** I like using a fine-point permanent marker to draw around the circle templates. It is easy to use on fabric, and the markings get lopped off when cutting.

* **Cutting Tools:** You need the usual quilters' cutting tools for cutting strips of fabric and batting: a rotary cutter, sharp blades, and a cutting mat. Use a 60mm cutter for batting—a 60mm blade cuts through two layers at a time, while a 45mm blade does not. Then cut the shapes from the strips using good fabric scissors; short scissors or nippers won't do.

* **Clips and Pins:** Use small to medium binder clips or small quilters' clips to hold the template onto the batting as you cut. Use a few flat-head pins when cutting circles. Use large quilting pins when folding FFHs. I prefer thin pins when folding FFHs and heavier pins to hold the toppers in place after folding.

* **Sewing Machine Feet:** If you're using a sewing machine, use the foot designated for zigzag or decorative stitching for both sewing the topper onto the base and for joining the hexies together. A walking foot is not necessary.

* **Work Surface:** You need a portable flat surface into which you can stick pins for the folding step of the hexies. Stack a few pieces of cardboard and tape them together, use an empty fabric bolt, or treat yourself and buy a deluxe folding surface: a piece of foam board.

Fast-Fold Hexie Construction

Making FFHs is actually pretty simple, once you've made a few. Refer to this section as you work on the projects in this book.

Preparing to Make Hexies

THE TEMPLATES

Trace and cut out the necessary templates (pages 101–106). Use paper or plastic for the circle templates and cardstock for the hexagon templates. Each project lists the specific templates needed, but in general you'll need a large circle template with the corresponding small circle and hexagon templates.

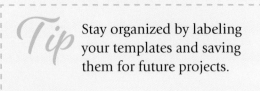

Tip Stay organized by labeling your templates and saving them for future projects.

CUTTING FABRIC

Cut strips of fabric with a rotary cutter, according to your project's directions. I find scissors quicker and easier to use when cutting circles and batting hexagons.

For circles 10" (25.4cm) and smaller, stack four or five layers of fabric, hold the fabric in place with flat-head pins, and place a plastic template on top. Use a fine-point permanent marker to trace around the circle template, then cut them out all at once.

Cut larger circles one at a time. Place the quarter-circle template on double-folded fabric, pin then cut out the circle.

CUTTING BATTING

If not using batting scraps, cut strips of batting with a 60mm rotary cutter and ruler. Batting hexagons can be cut two layers at a time. Align a straight edge from your template with a straight edge on your batting, if you have one. Use clips to hold the template in place as you cut. When cutting batting for the 5" (12.7cm) circle base, you do not need clips.

Clip the template to your batting and cut around each edge.

Cutting Tip You can cut up to two layers of batting at a time. I find scissors easier to use than a rotary cutter and rulers.

Folding the Hexies

THE BASE HEXIE

1. Cut out your fabric and batting using the appropriate templates. The FFH shown in this tutorial is made from a 10" (25.4cm) circle, a 5" (12.7cm) circle, and a piece of batting cut using the 5" (12.7cm) Hexagon Template.

2. Locate the center of the circle by folding the circle in half toward you, then finger-pressing the fold. Fold in half again and finger-press. Open the circle back up, keeping the fabric wrong side up.

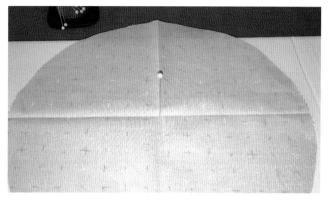

3. Place the 10" (25.4cm) circle wrong side up on your work surface, with the lengthwise grain of the fabric (the direction with the least give) running from top to bottom.

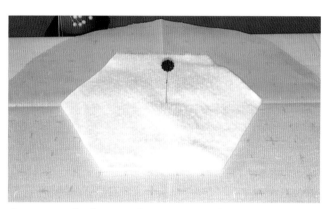

4. Center the batting hexagon on the circle as shown, matching the points with the horizontal fold line on the fabric. Place a pin through the center of the batting and fabric, and into the work surface.

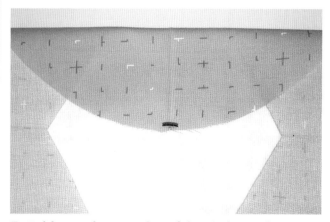

5. Fold over the top edge of the circle, as shown, so the fold meets the pin at the center. Finger-press the fold.

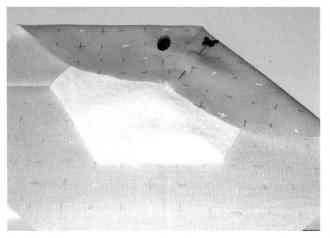

6. Working clockwise, bring the point created by the previous fold to the pin at the center, and finger-press. Pin in place to secure. Left-handed quilters may find it easier to work counterclockwise, folding to the left.

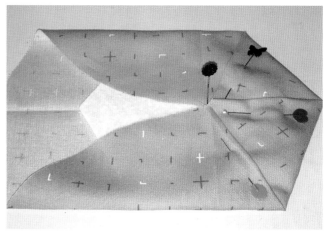

8. Repeat the same process as step 7. After this 4th fold, the long outside edges should be parallel. If not, open and fold again or adjust the last fold slightly.

7. Continuing to work counterclockwise, bring the next point to the center pin and finger-press in place. Pin to secure.

Folding Tip

If you're having trouble remembering what to do next, just think "point to the pin." The point created in the previous step gets folded into the center pin each time. Rotate your hexagon around the center pin as you fold, so that your hands are always in a comfortable position.

9. Continue folding, finger-pressing, and pinning until the final point is pinned in place. This completes the hexie base; set it aside as you fold the hexie topper.

THE TOPPER HEXIE

To fold the hexie topper, start with the 5" (12.7cm) circle and follow the steps for the hexie base, but omit the batting hexagon.

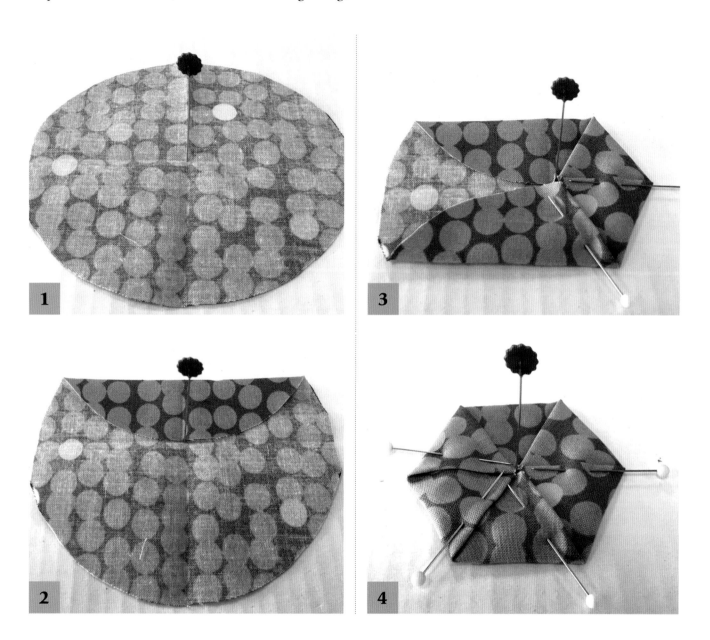

Assembling the Hexies

Place a hexie topper face down (folded side down) on a hexie base and pin it in place. Once everything is secure, you can remove the pins you used to hold the folds in place.

There are two options for placement: either line up the points on the hexie topper with the points on the base, or line up the points of the topper between the points on the base. Because of folding imperfections, I find it easier to align the topper points between the folds of the base.

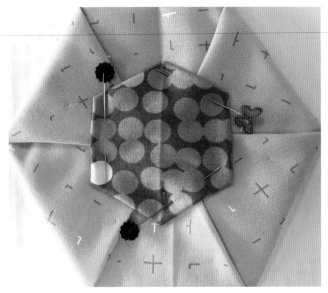

The topper is placed with the points between the base folds.

The topper is placed with the points aligned with the base folds.

1. Stitch the topper in place about ¼" (0.6cm) from the edge, using a straight, zigzag, buttonhole, or decorative stitch. Adjust your stitch length to be slightly longer than what you use for piecing to accommodate the thickness of the hexie unit.

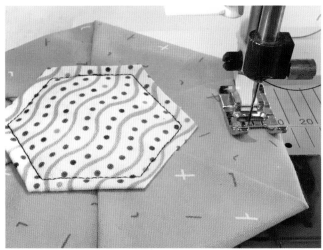

2. Stitch around the base hexie, about ⅜" from the edge, using a straight or decorative stitch. This holds the batting in place and serves as quilting for the unit.

Stitching Tip

Always test your zigzag or decorative stitch and adjust for length and width as needed.

1. To sew the topper by hand, thread a hand-sewing needle with one or two strands of thread. Knot your ends and bury the knot under the fold of the small hexagon. Sew a running stitch through all layers near the outside edge of the small hexagon, as shown. Tuck the thread between the layers and clip the thread to finish.

2. Sew another round of running stitches through all layers ⅜" (1cm) in from the edge of the base hexagon. Tuck the thread between the layers and clip the thread to finish.

Stitching Tip

Play with the type of stitches used (including decorative stitches) and the placement of those stitches when sewing around the toppers and bases.

Smaller hexies work well with stitching close to the edge; try ¼" (6mm) to start. Larger hexies can be stitched further from the edge. Remember that the purpose of the stitching is to secure the layers, but it can also add a decorative touch.

Detail of stitching on Fancy Stitches Table Topper, page 34).

Sewing the Hexie Units Together

MACHINE SEWING

Joining FFHs with a sewing machine allows you to use decorative or utility stitches. Select a stitch that sews from side to side so that the edge from each FFH is joined. I prefer the utility zigzag, also called a three-step zigzag. A regular zigzag or other decorative stitch can also be used. Adjust the width and length as needed.

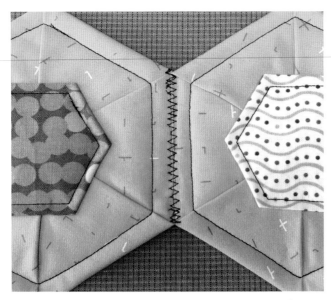

Joined FFHs. Note, black thread was used to make stitching visible.

Coordinating thread makes the stitching nearly invisible in these joined FFHs.

Before using any stitch, test it and consider the ease of sewing (for example, stitches that jump forward and back are harder to manage), time, and thread quantity. Normally, a coordinating thread is used to sew the FFHs together, so any irregularities in stitching are not obvious.

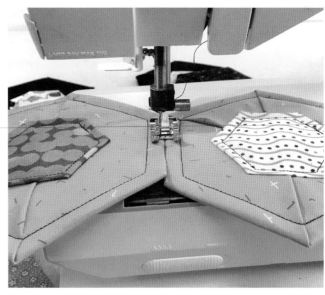

Position the FFHs to be joined under the presser foot, aligning the center of the presser foot with the point where the FFHs adjoin.

To sew two FFHs together, butt two flat edges together and position them under your presser foot. For my machine, keeping the middle of the presser foot aligned with the point where the FFHs butt together worked best, but this may vary by machine. Make sure your stitch is catching each edge and add a few backstitches at the beginning and end of the seam to secure.

SEWING BY HAND

Position your hexies right side together, and clip or pin in place. Using a single strand of thread, bury the knot near your starting position, and whipstitch the hexies together. Keep your stitches small and add a few reinforcing stitches at the beginning and end of the seam. Bury the thread and clip away the tail.

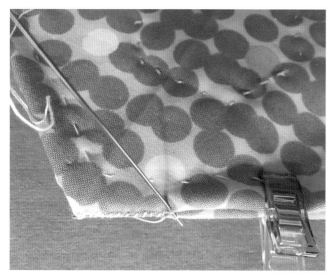

Whipstitch the hexies together by hand.

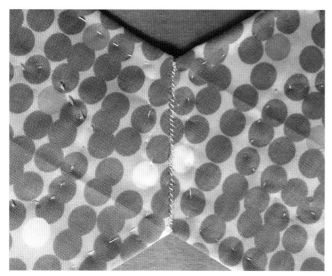

Completed whipstitched seam; note that a heavier thread is used to show the stitching.

Stitching Tip

When joining FFHs together, standard-weight thread usually used for piecing will blend in to your fabric as you stitch. A single strand of 80–100wt thread however, will make the stitches nearly invisible.

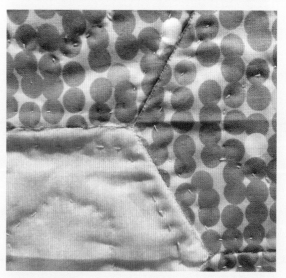

Whipstitches done with 80–100wt thread are nearly invisible.

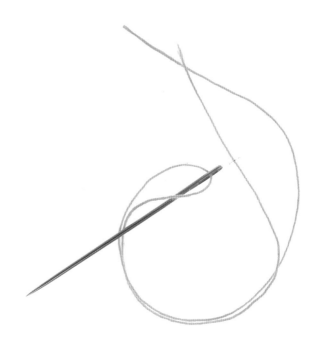

Joining Layouts

While each project in this book gives specific directions on the order in which to join FFHs, there are two main methods: sewing in columns or sewing in the round.

THE COLUMN METHOD

To follow this method, first join your FFHs into columns, then join the columns from left to right.

First join the single columns, then join the columns together. The red lines indicate stitching lines.

THE ROUNDS METHOD

For the rounds method, first join your hexies into a circle and then join the center unit. As you make additional rounds, you'll complete the next circle, then join the previous unit in the center.

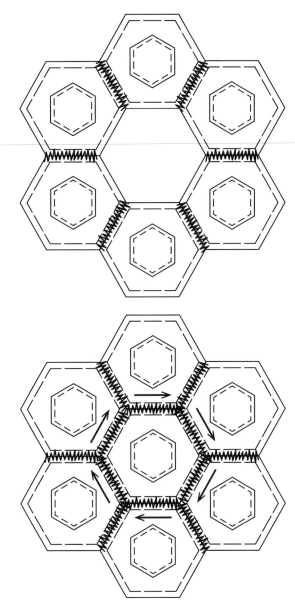

First join the hexies in a round, then add the center or previous unit.

UNDERSTANDING THE STRAIGHT OF GRAIN

The "envelope" is the section of the base hexagon between your first and last folds, as indicated by arrows in photo to the right. The folds face each other. When joining hexie units together, keeping all the envelopes oriented in the same direction will maintain your straight of grain.

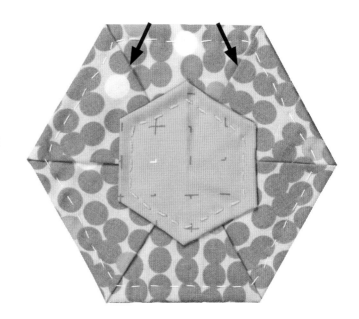

Tips for Large Projects

Over the years, I've developed some tips for sewing large FFH projects:

✳ **Take your time.** There's no rush to finish, so don't feel you have to finish joining all the columns or rounds in one sitting.

✳ **Find a larger workspace.** A larger than usual workspace can help support the weight and bulk of the quilt.

Above: Author Mary Hogan sewing a large FFH quilt at her machine.

Making and Using Half Hexagons

Half hexagons are useful for filling the edges of FFH quilts, usually along the top and bottom edges. While none of the projects in this book use half hexies, you may want to use them. The process for making a half FFH is very similar to that of a full FFH, with two key differences: the batting is cut in half, and whole hexie is folded in half before stitching the base.

MAKING HALF FAST-FOLD HEXIES

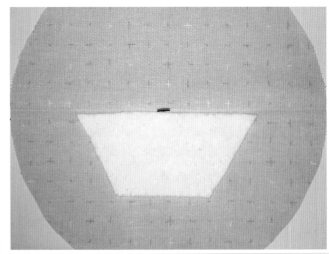

2. Place your batting below the pin and, in the same manner as a regular FFH (page 11), pin and finger-press as you work around the circle.

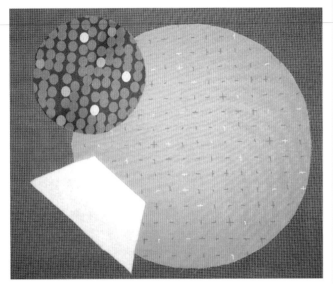

1. Gather your materials: a base circle, a topper circle, and a half hexagon of batting. Fold to find the center of the base circle and pin at the center.

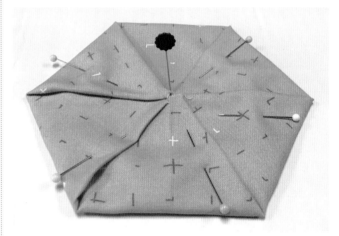

The folded half FFH looks the same as any other FFH, but there is no batting under the top half.

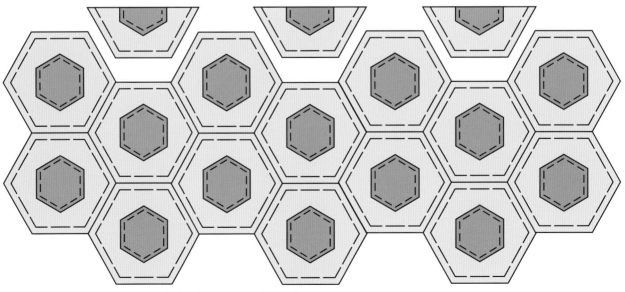

You can use half hexagons to fill in the edges of a quilt.

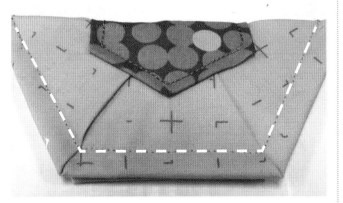

3. Fold the topper, using the same method as a regular FFH (page 13), and sew it in place.

4. Fold the hexie in half, from corner to corner, and sew around the 3 edges, as shown.

JOINING HALF FAST-FOLD HEXIES

Half FFHs should be added to the correct column before joining the columns together. Use a zigzag stitch or your preferred joining stitch to sew the hexies together.

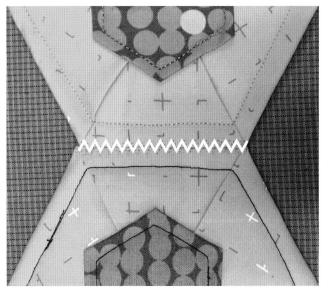

The zigzag line shows where the hexies are joined.

Advantages of the Fast-Fold Method

Once you understand the process for making fast-fold hexies, you can appreciate some of the advantages of this technique.

✳ **Works well with precuts.** Using precut fabrics will save you time, and most of the projects in this book are precut friendly. Cut 10" (25.4cm) and 5" (12.7cm) circles from 10" (25.4cm) and 5" (12.7cm) square precuts. Fat quarters (18" x 21" [45.7 x 53.3cm]) can be used for 18" (45.7cm) circle base projects, and 10" (25.4cm) precut squares can be used for the coordinating 9" (22.9cm) circle toppers.

✳ **Use up your stash.** Whether your stash is full of small scraps, which work great for the 2½" (6.4cm) circle toppers, or large pieces of yardage, you probably already have a lot of fabric you can use for these projects.

✳ **Use up batting scraps.** There aren't many projects that make use of small batting scraps, but FFHs do. Use leftover pieces to cut out your batting hexagons.

✳ **Portable and varied projects.** Once a few bases, toppers, and batting hexagons are cut, these

Make a beautiful, one-of-a-kind quilt from scraps as seen in Anything Goes Scrap Quilt (page 74).

Intersecting Shapes Quilt (page 60); edge of quilt requires no binding.

The back of the Pathways Quilt (page 66) is a work of art in itself.

projects are perfectly portable. Fold up some hexies while relaxing on the couch or when you're on the road. You can bring everything you need to fold and stitch the hexies by hand.

✳ **Do the quilting yourself.** Because you're quilting as you go, you don't have to worry about the extra fee for sending your quilt out to be quilted. Plus, you don't have to spend time making a quilt sandwich—the batting and backing are already done.

✳ **No binding needed.** The finished edges of the FFHs eliminate the need for a separate binding step.

✳ **The backs are beautiful.** Because the individual hexies are joined, you see the stitching and hexie shape on both sides of the quilt.

THE PROJECTS

The projects in this book range from very simple (e.g., Seven-Hexie Trivet, page 32) to more complex and time-consuming (e.g., Anything Goes Quilt, page 74). I recommend you start small and go from there.

The book provides only some examples of what might be made with FFHs. Once you get the hang of it, use some of the resources provided to design and make your own FFH projects.

Small Pouch

This small pouch requires only two FFHs with 7" (12.7cm) base hexies. The size is perfect for holding pocket change, but you can easily adjust the size by making larger or smaller hexies, I love making these; they are quick, are lined, and have finished edges.

Finished Size: 3½" x 4" (8.9 x 10.2cm)

Materials

- Scrap fabric
- Scraps of batting
- Small piece of hook-and-loop tape, iron-on or sew-in
- 7" (17.8cm) Circle Template
- 3½" (8.9cm) Circle Template
- 3½" (8.9cm) Hexagon Template

Cutting

From the scrap fabric, cut:
- (2) 7" (17.8cm) circles
- (2) 3½" (8.9cm) circles

From the batting, cut:
- 2 pieces using the 3½" (8.9cm) Hexagon Template

1. Make the FFHs. Prepare 2 FFHs following the instructions on page 11. Each FFH requires a base, a topper, and batting.

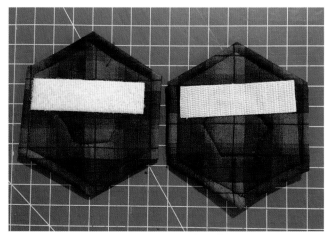

2. Add hook-and-loop tape. Lay out the hook-and-loop tape as shown. If using iron-on tape, follow the product directions for adhering the tape in place. Use parchment paper or a pressing cloth to prevent scorching the fabric. Alternatively, use sew-on hook-and-loop tape and stitch in place.

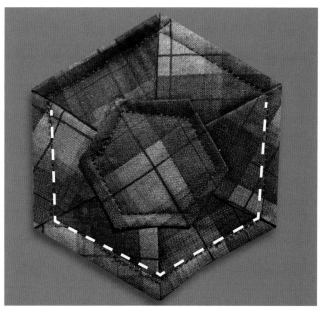

3. Assemble the pouch. Place the 2 FFHs wrong sides together, matching the location of the hook-and-loop tape. Sew the outside edges, leaving the sides above the hook-and-loop tape open. The dashed line shows where you should stitch the pouch.

Pouch Variations

You can never have too many pouches! Try adding a ring, twill tape, or even a wrist handle. Use contrasting fabrics for your hexie topper and base, or keep them both the same. You can even try fussy-cutting your fabric for added detail (page 94).

Zippered Pencil Case

Makeup bag, pencil pouch, notions bag—you'll find plenty of reasons to make this versatile pouch. Because of the unique construction of the fast-fold hexies, the inside of the bag is fully finished; no separate lining required!

Finished size: 10" x 6½" (25.4 x 16.5cm)

Materials

- Scraps of batting
- 2 fat quarters
- 10" (25.4cm) zipper
- 7" (17.8cm) Circle Template
- 3½" (8.9cm) Circle Template
- 3½" (8.9cm) Hexagon Template

Cutting

From the batting, cut:
- 12 pieces using the 3½" (8.9cm) Hexagon Template

From the fat quarters, cut:
- (12) 7" (17.8cm) circles, 6 from each fat quarter
- (12) 3½" (8.9cm) circles, 6 from each fat quarter

Cutting From Fat Quarters

To cut 7" (17.8cm) and 3½" (8.9cm) circles, fold the fat quarters into thirds, 18" x 7" (45.7 x 17.8cm). Position the larger circle template on the far left, and cut through 3 layers of fabric to get 3 large circles. Repeat on the far right of the fat quarter. Cut sets of 3½" (8.9cm) circles from the rest of the fabric.

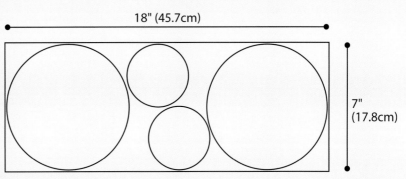

18" (45.7cm)

7" (17.8cm)

Instructions

1. Make the FFHs. Prepare 12 FFHs following the instructions on page 11. Each FFH requires a base, topper, and batting.

2. Join the FFHs. Lay out the hexie units as shown in columns of 6. Be sure to keep the lengthwise straight of grain for each base hexagon oriented in the same direction; that is, with the envelope to the top (page 19). Following the instructions on page 16, sew the units together in each column, starting at the top, and working your way down. Then sew the 2 columns.

3. Sew the side seam. Fold the pouch in half wrong sides out, as shown, and sew the side seam by hand.

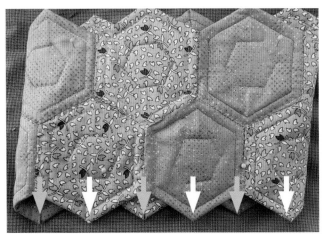

4. Sew the bottom. With the pouch still wrong sides out, arrange the points along the bottom edge so that they are staggered, with the points in the front (white arrows) between the points in the back (gray arrows).

Carefully pick up and start hand sewing the bottom shut, starting at the middle and working your way out to the edge. Keep the points nestled into the corners.

5. As you get to the end of one side, you'll have three edges. Sew the two flat edges together as shown (the white lines), and fold the third edge in half (red line), then sew. Repeat, starting at the center and working to the other edge of the pouch.

6. Add the zipper. Turn the pouch right sides out and use your hands to flatten the edges. Mark the side folds with pins along the top edge, and use pins to secure the entire pouch along the bottom.

Pin the zipper to the inside of both long sides of the pouch. It should be placed under the points that stick up.

Working from the top side of the zipper, whipstitch along the full length of the zipper, using small stitches. Adjust the pins if needed. Sew the other side of the zipper into place the same way.

Handbag Variation

By using the same construction method but increasing the number of FFHs in each column and adding more columns, you can create a larger version of the pencil case. Swap out the zipper for leather straps and you have made a handbag.

Seven-Hexie Trivet

A perfect beginner project, this simple trivet mixes machine sewing on the toppers and hand quilting at the edge of the base hexies. The individual FFHs are also sewn together by hand, though you can use machine stitching for the entire project.

Finished size: 14½" x 15" (36.8 x 38.1cm)

Materials

Note: Fabric requirements are based on 42" (106.7cm) wide fabric. WOF = width of fabric.

- ¼ yard (23cm) of 90" (2.3m) wide batting
- ⅝ yard (57cm) gray print fabric for the base hexies and center topper
- ¼ yard (23cm) yellow fabric for the toppers and center base
- 10" (25.4cm) Circle Template
- 5" (12.7cm) Circle Template
- 5" (12.7cm) Hexagon Template

Cutting

From the batting, cut:
- 7 pieces using the 5" (12.7cm) Hexagon Template

From the gray print fabric, cut:
- (2) 10" (25.4cm) x WOF strips. From these cut (6) 10" (25.4cm) circles. Each strip yields 4 circles.
- Cut (1) 5" (12.7cm) circle

From the yellow fabric, cut:
- Cut (1) 10" (25.4cm) circle
- Cut (6) 5" (12.7cm) circles

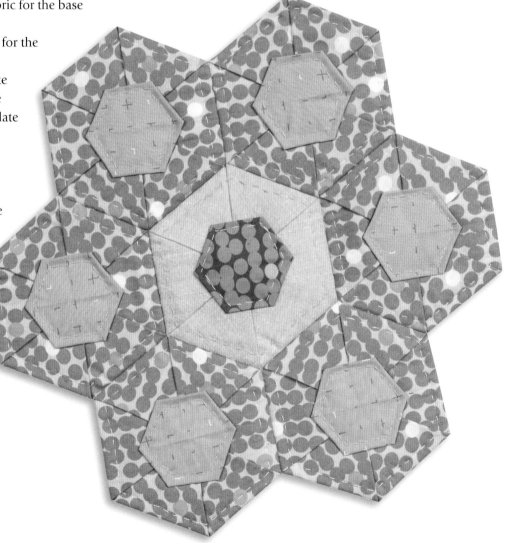

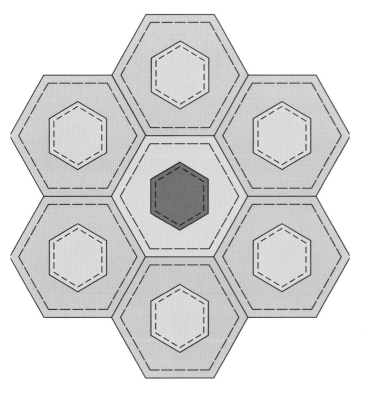

Layout Diagram

Instructions

1. Make the FFHs. Using the instructions on page 11, construct 7 FFHs. Machine stitch the toppers in place, but use hand quilting to finish the stitching around the bases.

2. Join the FFHs. Lay out the hexie units as shown. Following the instructions on page 16, sew the units together by first joining the outer circle, then adding the center unit. You can stitch by hand or machine.

Fabric Tips

In the sample shown, I used a different fabric for the center topper. If you have fabric scraps lying around, try using something different for the center topper.

Trivet Variations

By changing up your fabrics and experimenting with fussy cutting, you can create a dramatically different trivet.

Fussy cutting the toppers makes the flowers the focus of this trivet.

Fancy Stitches Table Topper

I designed this project to experiment with different thread colors and decorative stitches. The added detail makes it fun to stitch. Alternating light and dark fabrics highlights the rounds. Use precut squares to make the fabric selection and cutting easier.

Finished size: 31" x 40" (0.79 x 1.02m)

Materials

- ⅝ yard (57.1cm) of 90" (2.3m) wide batting
- (2) 10" (25.4cm) precut squares bright fabric (for center hexies)
- (28) 10" (25.4cm) precut squares assorted light fabrics
- (22) 10" (25.4cm) precut squares assorted dark fabrics
- (2) 5" (12.7cm) precut squares assorted bright fabrics (for center hexies)
- (28) 5" (12.7cm) precut squares light fabric
- (22) 5" (12.7cm) precut squares dark fabric
- 10" (25.4cm) Circle Template
- 5" (12.7cm) Circle Template
- 5" (12.7cm) Hexagon Template

Cutting

From the batting, cut:
- (3) 6½" (16.5cm) strips of 90" (2.3m) wide batting. From these, cut 44 pieces using the 5" (12.7cm) Hexagon Template. Each batting strip yields 15 hexagons

From the bright fabric (center hexies), cut:
- (2) 10" (25.4cm) circles
- (2) 5" (12.7cm) circles

From the light fabric (rounds 1 and 3), cut:
- (28) 10" (25.4cm) circles
- (28) 5" (12.7cm) circles

From the dark fabric (round 2), cut:
- (22) 10" (25.4cm) circles
- (22) 5" (12.7cm) circles

Instructions

1. **Make the FFHs.** Prepare, fold, and quilt 2 bright FFHs for the center, 8 light FFHs for round 1, 14 dark FFHs for round 2, and 20 light FFHs for round 3 (44 FFHs total) following the instructions on page 11. Use a variety of decorative stitches.

2. **Join the FFHs.** Lay out the hexies using the diagrams provided. Sew the center hexies together and set aside. Sew the round 1 hexies together, then place round 1 around the center unit and sew it in place. Continue working this manner, joining the hexies for the next round before joining the round to the center unit.

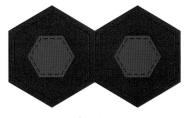

Center

Assembly Note

If you prefer sewing in columns, adjust the layout and join your hexies that way instead.

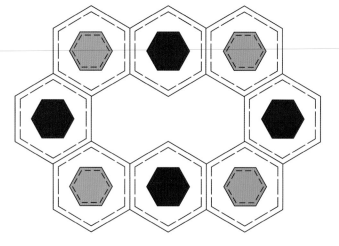

Round 1

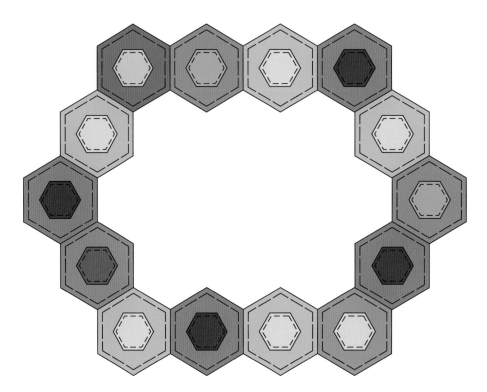

Round 2

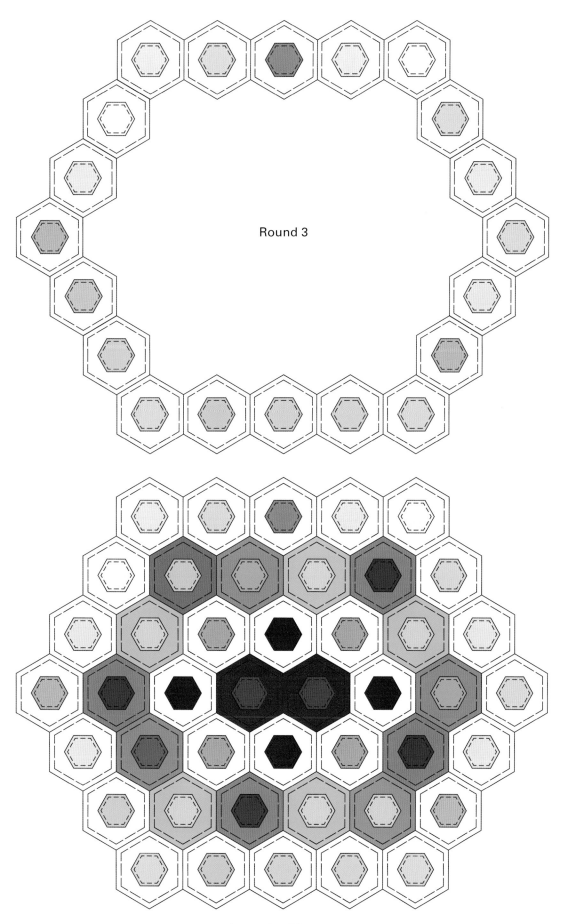

Round 3

Assembly Diagram

Quilters Love Color
Bed Runner

This project is inspired by fat-quarter bundles that included fabrics ranging from light to dark value within a single color. The resulting project is a study in color and value. In each section, a central white hexagon is surrounded by three rings of progressively darker color. White FFHs are used to surround and join each section. This project works equally well as a bed runner or a wall hanging.

Finished size: 45" x 74" (1.14 x 1.88m)

Materials

Note: Fabric requirements are based on 42" (106.7cm) wide fabric. WOF = width of fabric.
- 1¼ yards (1.2m) of 90" (2.3m) wide batting
- 3⅛ yards (2.9m) of white fabric

For each colored section (red, orange, and yellow) you need:
- 1 light-value fat quarter
- 2 medium-value fat quarters
- 3 dark-value fat quarters
- 7" (17.8cm) Circle Template
- 3½" (8.9cm) Circle Template
- 3½" (8.9cm) Hexagon Template

Cutting Tip

Use the diagram on page 29 to cut your circles from the fat quarters.

Cutting

From the batting, cut:
- (9) 5" (12.7cm) strips of 90" (2.3m) wide batting. From these, cut (173) pieces using the 3½" (8.9cm) Hexagon Template. Each batting strip yields 21 hexagons

From the white fabric, cut:
- (11) 7" (17.8cm) x WOF strips of fabric. From these strips cut (65) 7" (17.8cm) circles. Each strip yields 6 circles
- (6) 3½" (8.9cm) x WOF strips of fabric. From these strips, cut (65) 3½" (8.9cm) circles. Each strip yields 12 circles

Note: Use the following cutting instructions for each of the 3 colorways.

From the light-colored fat quarters, cut:
- (6) 7" (17.8cm) circles
- (6) 3½" (8.9cm) circles

From the medium-colored fat quarters, cut:
- (12) 7" (17.8cm) circles
- (12) 3½" (8.9cm) circles

From the dark-colored fat quarters, cut:
- (18) 7" circles (17.8cm)
- (18) 3½" (8.9cm) circles

Instructions

1. Make the FFHs. Fold the required number of FFHs for each colorway, following the instructions on page 11. I used decorative stitching to sew the toppers in place. If you use decorative stitching, omit the final row of stitching around the base hexie so that the decorative stitching is the star.

For each colored unit, you need:
* 1 white hexagon for center
* 6 light-value hexagons (round 1); use light- and medium-value toppers
* 12 medium-value hexagons (round 2); use light- to dark-value toppers
* 18 dark-value hexagons (round 3); use light- to dark-value toppers

For joining, you need:
* 62 white hexagons with white toppers

2. Join the FFHs. Start with a single colorway. As the FFHs are laid out, keep the lengthwise straight of grain for each base hexagon oriented in the same direction; in this case, with the envelopes to the left (page 19).

Using the diagrams, lay out and sew the FFHs for round 1, then sew the center FFH in place. Lay out and sew the FFHs in round 2 together. Place round 2 around the previously completed section and sew into place. Lay out and sew the FFHs in round 3 together. Place round 3 around the previously completed section and sew into place. Sew the background section together, place it around the completed section, and sew in place.

Repeat this process until you have all 3 color units assembled. Sew the remaining 5 white FFHs into a single row.

3. Assemble the runner. Following the Assembly Diagram, sew the strip of white hexies onto the topmost (red) section, as shown. Sew the middle (orange) section to the top, then join the bottom (yellow) section.

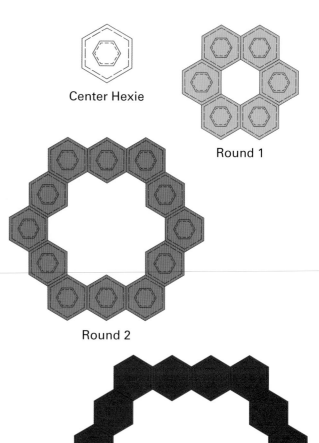

Center Hexie

Round 1

Round 2

Round 3

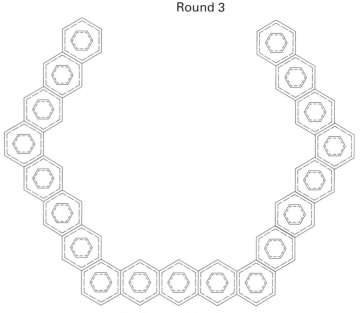

Background Hexies

Assembly Diagram

Holiday Tree Skirt

Leftover scraps of holiday fabric work great for this tree skirt. The skirt is constructed much like previous projects, except the center is left open, and the rounds are left unjoined, so you can place the skirt around a tree. If you prefer a table topper, simply add a center unit, and join the rounds.

Finished size: 38" x 45" (0.97 x 1.14m)

Materials

Note: Fabric requirements are based on 42" (106.7cm) wide fabric. WOF = width of fabric.

- ¾ yard (68.6cm) of 90" (2.3m) wide batting
- ⅝ yard (57.2cm) white print fabric (fabric A)
- ¾ yard (68.6cm) red blender fabric (fabric B)
- ⅞ yard (80cm) black print fabric (fabric C)
- ⅜ yard (34.3cm) dark olive fabric (fabric D)
- 1⅜ yards (1.26m) red dotted fabric (fabric E)
- ½ yard (45.7cm) green print fabric (fabric F)
- 1¾ yards (1.6m) white print fabric (fabric G)
- 10" (25.4cm) Circle Template
- 5" (12.7cm) Circle Template
- 5" (12.7cm) Hexagon Template

Cutting

From the batting, cut:

- (4) 6½" (16.5cm) strips of 90" (2.3m) wide batting. From these strips, cut 60 pieces using the 5" (12.7cm) Hexagon Template. Each batting strip yields 15 hexagons

From fabric A, cut:

- (2) 10" (25.4cm) x WOF strips of fabric. From these strips cut (6) 10" (25.4cm) circles. Each strip yields 4 circles

From fabric B, cut:

- (4) 5" (12.7cm) x WOF strips of fabric. From these strips cut (30) 5" (12.7cm) circles. Each strip yields 8 circles

From fabric C, cut:

- (3) 10" (25.4cm) x WOF strips of fabric. From these strips cut (12) 10" (25.4cm) circles. Each strip yields 4 circles

From fabric D, cut:

- (2) 5" (12.7cm) x WOF strips of fabric. From these strips cut (12) 5" (12.7cm) circles. Each strip yields 8 circles

From fabric E, cut:

- (5) 10" (25.4cm) x WOF strips of fabric. From these strips cut (18) 10" (25.4cm) circles. Each strip yields 4 circles

From fabric F, cut:

- (3) 5" (12.7cm) x WOF strips of fabric. From these strips cut (18) 5" (12.7cm) circles. Each strip yields 8 circles

From fabric G, cut:

- (6) 10" (25.4cm) x WOF strips of fabric. From these strips cut (24) 10" (25.4cm) circles. Each strip yields 4 circles

Instructions

1. Make the FFHs. Prepare a total of 60 FFHs, following the instructions on page 11.

For round 1, make:
* 6 fabric A bases with fabric B toppers

For round 2, make:
* 12 fabric C bases with fabric D toppers

For round 3, make:
* 18 fabric E bases with fabric F toppers

For round 4, make:
* 24 fabric G bases with fabric B toppers

2. Join the FFHs. Lay out the FFHs in rounds, using the Assembly Diagram as a guide. Sew round 1 FFHs together, leaving one join open. Do the same for rounds 2, 3, and 4, joining each subsequent round to the previous unit as you go.

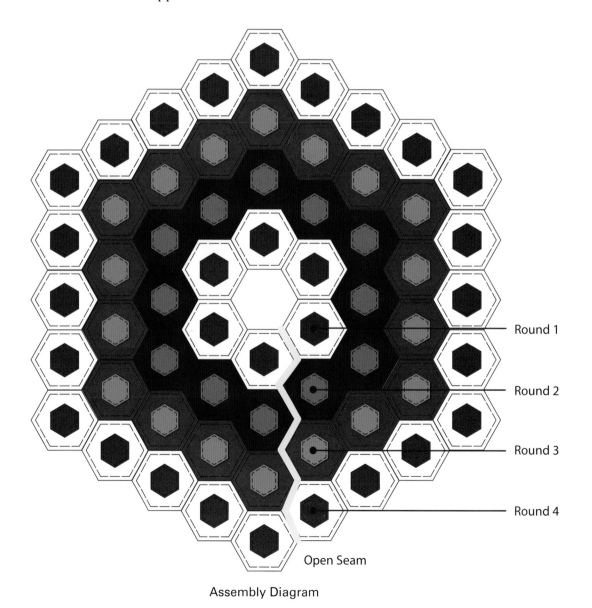

Round 1
Round 2
Round 3
Round 4

Open Seam

Assembly Diagram

Holiday Wall Hanging

This quick tree wall hanging is a great decoration for the holidays, and it's easy to take down once the holidays are over. Keep it simple and let the fabric be the star, or have fun with decorating: buttons, beads, and trim are all festive additions.

Finished size: 20" x 23" (51 x 58cm)

Materials

Note: Fabric requirements are based on 42" (106.7cm) wide fabric. WOF = width of fabric.
- ¼ yard (22.9cm) of 90" (2.3m) wide batting
- ⅞ yard (80cm) green blender fabric
- ⅜ yard (34.3cm) holiday print fabric
- (1) 10" (25.4cm) square and (1) 5" (12.7cm) square brown fabric
- Buttons, beads, and trim (optional)
- Small amount of ribbon (optional)
- 10" (25.4cm) Circle Template
- 5" (12.7cm) Circle Template
- 5" (12.7cm) Hexagon Template

Cutting

From the batting, cut:
- (1) 6½" (16.5cm) strip of 90" (2.3m) wide batting. From this strip, cut 11 pieces using the 5" (12.7cm) Hexagon Template. Each batting strip yields 15 hexagons

From the green fabric, cut:
- (3) 10" (25.4cm) x WOF strips of fabric. From these strips cut (10) 10" (25.4cm) circles. Each strip yields 4 circles

From the holiday print fabric, cut:
- (2) 5" (12.7cm) x WOF strips of fabric. From these strips cut (10) 5" (12.7cm) circles. Each strip yields 8 circles

From the brown fabric, cut:
- (1) 10" (25.4cm) circle
- (1) 5" (12.7cm) circle

Instructions

1. Make the FFHs. Prepare a total of 11 FFHs, following the instructions on page 11. Make 10 hexagons with green bases and holiday print toppers, and 1 hexagon with a brown base and brown topper.

2. Join the FFHs. Arrange the FFHs as shown, keeping the lengthwise straight of grain oriented in the same direction (page 19). Join the hexies for column 2, 3, and 4 using the method described on page 16.

3. Assemble the tree. Join column 1 (the trunk) to column 2, using your selected joining stitch. Add column 3 to the joined unit, then add column 4 and finally, column 5.

4. Add embellishments. Sew on buttons, beads, and trim as desired. Sew a ribbon loop to the top hexagon for hanging.

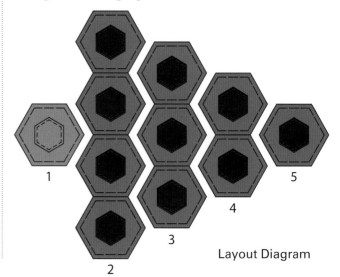

Layout Diagram

Single Hexie Pot Holder

A single large FFH and several layers of batting make a quick trivet, hot pad, or mug mat. This trivet uses a leftover piece of home décor fabric, but quilting cotton works, too. I used two layers of Warm & Natural cotton batting, but you can use a layer of heat-resistant batting if you like. Consider adding a loop if you plan on using this as a hot pad.

Finished Size: 9" x 10½" (22.9 x 26.7cm)

Materials

- 1 fat-quarter or 18" (45.7cm) square quilting cotton or home décor fabric
- 9" (22.9cm) square topper fabric
- 2 pieces of scrap batting, each 9" (22.8cm) x 10½" (26.7cm) (heat-resistant batting is optional)
- 18" (45.7cm) Circle Template
- 9" (22.9cm) Circle Template
- 9" (22.9cm) Hexagon Template

Cutting

From the fat-quarter, cut:
- (1) 18" (45.7cm) circle

From the topper fabric, cut:
- (1) 9" (22.9cm) circle

From the batting, cut:
- 2 pieces using the 9" Hexagon Template

Instructions

1. Make the FFH. Fold and assemble the hexie following the instructions on page 11. Double the batting and fold the fabric around both pieces as you go for added insulation.

2. Quilt the FFH. Add additional quilting lines around the hexie as desired.

Right side of coaster.

Wrong side of coaster.

Coaster Variation

A single FFH in a smaller size can also work as a coaster. Add decorative quilting lines to give the coaster more detail.

Yellow, Gray, and Black Baby Quilt

Yellow, black, and white are the perfect combination of cheery colors for this quilt. The size works well either as a baby quilt or a lap quilt. While I prefer to assemble this quilt in rounds, you can assemble it column by column, if you prefer.

Finished size: 36" x 45" (91 x 114cm)

Materials

Note: Fabric requirements are based on 42" (106.7cm) wide fabric. WOF = width of fabric.

- 1⅛ yards (103cm) of 90" (2.3m) wide batting
- (1) 10" (25.4cm) square and (1) 5" (12.7cm) square dark gray fabric (fabric A)
- ⅝ yard (57.2cm) assorted yellow print fabrics (fabric B)
- ¼ yard (23cm) assorted gray print fabrics (fabric C)
- ⅞ yard (80cm) assorted black print fabrics (fabric D)
- ⅜ yard (34.3cm) assorted black on white print fabrics (fabric E)
- 1½ yards (1.4m) assorted black-and-white polka dot fabrics (fabric F)
- ½ yard (45.7cm) assorted yellow fabrics (fabric G)
- 2⅞ yards (2.6m) assorted yellow print fabrics (fabric H)
- ¾ yard (68.6cm) assorted black on white print fabrics (fabric I)
- 10" (25.4cm) Circle Template
- 5" (12.7cm) Circle Template
- 5" (12.7cm) Hexagon Template

Cutting

From the batting, cut:
- (6) 6½" (16.5cm) strips of 90" (2.3m) wide batting. From these strips, cut 77 pieces using the 5" (12.7cm) Hexagon Template. Each batting strip yields 15 hexagons

From fabric A, cut:
- (1) 10" (25.4cm) circle
- (1) 5" (12.7cm) circle

From fabric B, cut:
- (2) 10" (25.4cm) x WOF strips of fabric. From these strips, cut (6) 10" (25.4cm) circles. Each strip yields 4 circles

From fabric C, cut:
- (1) 5" (12.7cm) x WOF strips of fabric. From this strip, cut (6) 5" (12.7cm) circles. Each strip yields 8 circles

From fabric D, cut:
- (3) 10" (25.4cm) x WOF strips of fabric. From these strips, cut (12) 10" (25.4cm) circles. Each strip yields 4 circles

From fabric E, cut:
- (2) 5" (12.7cm) x WOF strips of fabric. From these strips, cut (12) 5" (12.7cm) circles. Each strip yields 8 circles

From fabric F, cut:
- (5) 10" (25.4cm) x WOF strips of fabric. From these strips, cut (18) 10" (25.4cm) circles. Each strip yields 4 circles

From fabric G, cut:
- (3) 5" (12.7cm) x WOF strips of fabric. From this strip, cut (18) 5" (12.7cm) circles. Each strip yields 8 circles

From fabric H, cut:
- (10) 10" (25.4cm) x WOF strips of fabric. From these strips, cut (40) 10" (25.4cm) circles. Each strip yields 4 circles

From fabric I, cut:
- (5) 5" (12.7cm) x WOF strips of fabric. From these strips, cut (40) 5" (12.7cm) circles. Each strip yields 8 circles

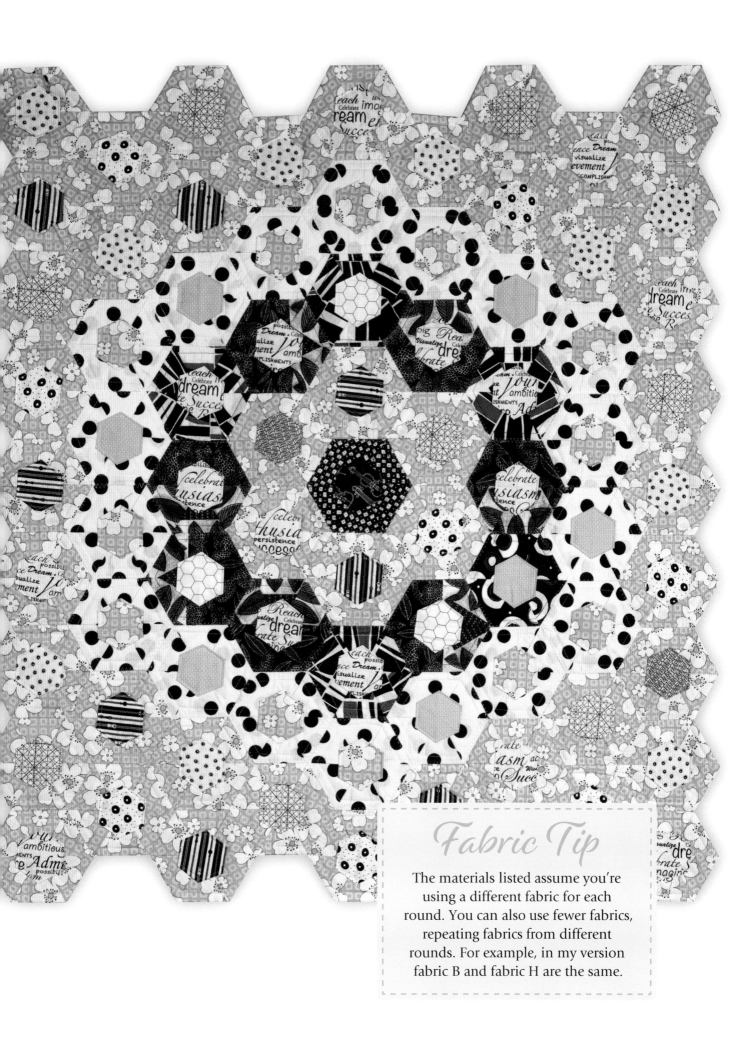

Instructions

1. Make the FFHs. Make the following FFHs, following the instructions on page 11.

For the center, make:
✳ 1 FFH with fabric A

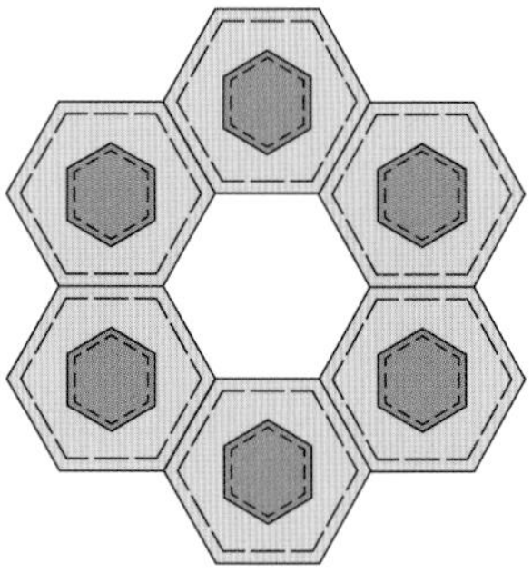

For round 1, make:
✳ 6 FFHs with fabric B bases and fabric C toppers

For round 2, make:
✳ 12 FFHs with fabric D bases and fabric E toppers

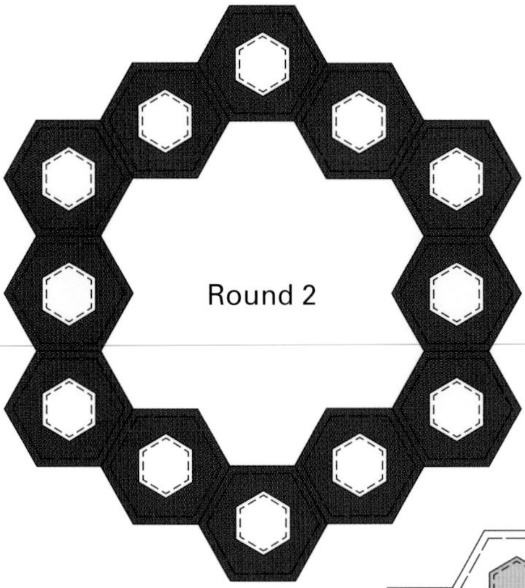

For round 3, make:
✳ 18 FFHs with fabric F bases and fabric G toppers

For round 4 and corners, make:
✳ 40 FFHs with fabric H bases and fabric I toppers

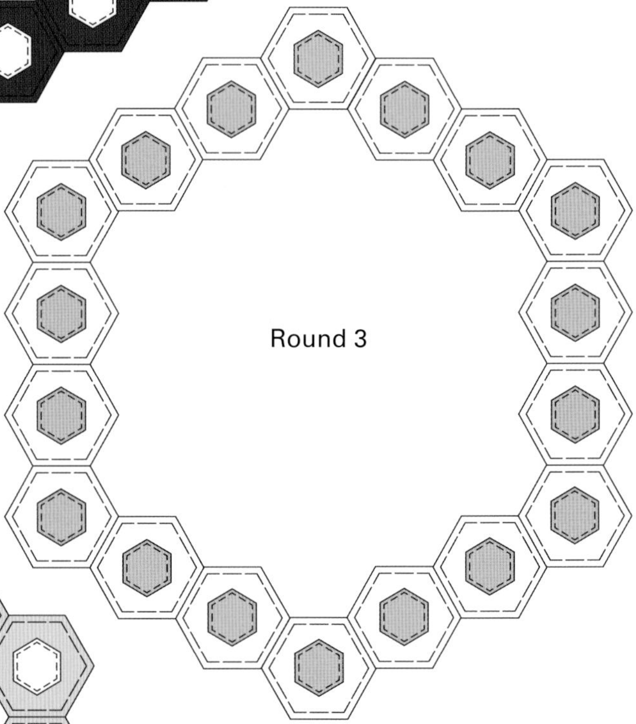

2. Join the FFHs. Arrange the FFHs in rounds as shown, keeping the lengthwise straight of grain oriented in the same direction (page 19). The hexies are joined in rounds, using the method described on page 18.

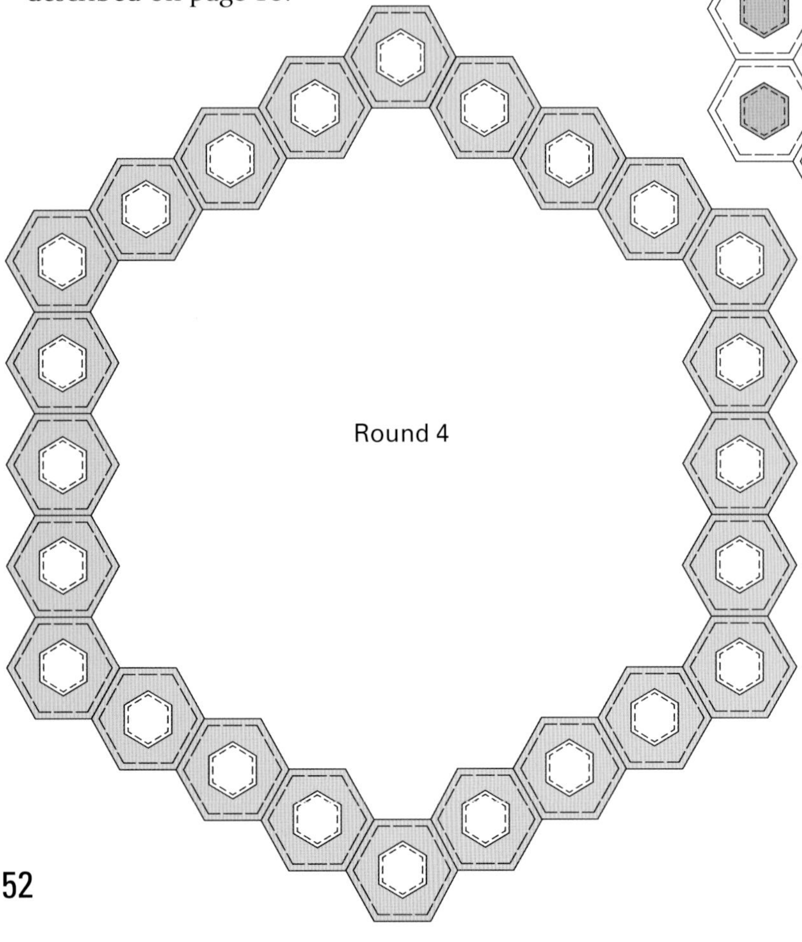

Center Hexie

Round 1

Round 2

Round 3

Round 4

Sew round 1 FFHs together, then place the round around the center FFH and join. Do the same for rounds 2, 3, and 4, joining each subsequent round to the center unit as you go.

Join the hexies for the corner units, noting that they are not all the same. Join the corners to the quilt as shown.

Four Corner
Units

Assembly Diagram

Dot-Dot-Dot Baby Quilt

Dot-Dot-Dot uses the same fabric for all the base hexagons, with varying solids and blenders for the toppers. The toppers appear to be large dots against the background fabric. This size is perfect for baby or lap quilts.

Finished size: 40" x 45" (0.91 x 1.14m)

Materials

Note: Fabric requirements are based on 42" (106.7cm) wide fabric. WOF = width of fabric.
- 1⅛ yards (1.03m) of 90" (2.3m) wide batting
- 6 yards (5.5m) background fabric
- 1¾ yards (1.6m) assorted solids and blenders
- 10" (25.4cm) Circle Template
- 5" (12.7cm) Circle Template
- 5" (12.7cm) Hexagon Template

Cutting

From the batting, cut:
- (6) 6½" (16.5cm) strips of 90" (2.3m) wide batting. From these strips, cut 81 pieces using the 5" (12.7cm) Hexagon Template. Each batting strip yields 15 hexagons

From the background fabric, cut:
- Cut (21) 10" (25.4cm) x WOF strips. From these strips, cut (81) 10" (25.4cm) circles. Each strip yields 4 circles

From the assorted solids and blenders:
- Cut (11) 5" (12.7cm) x WOF strips. From these strips, cut (81) 5" (12.7cm) circles. Each strip yields 8 circles

Instructions

1. Make the FFHs. Following the instructions on page 11, make 81 FFHs.

2. Lay out the columns. Arrange the FFHs as shown in the Layout Diagram, laying out the hexies in columns. Keep the lengthwise straight of grain for each base hexagon oriented the same way (page 19). Label the columns to keep them organized, then sew the FFHs in each column together, following the instructions on page 16.

3. Join the columns. Sew column 2 to column 1 using your selected joining stitch, then attach column 3 to column 2. Next, sew columns 4 and 5 together, then sew columns 6 and 7 together, and, finally, sew columns 8 and 9 together.

Working from left to right, join all units together.

Assembly Note

For this project, the toppers are oriented the same direction as the bases so that the points match. Feel free to orient the toppers however you prefer.

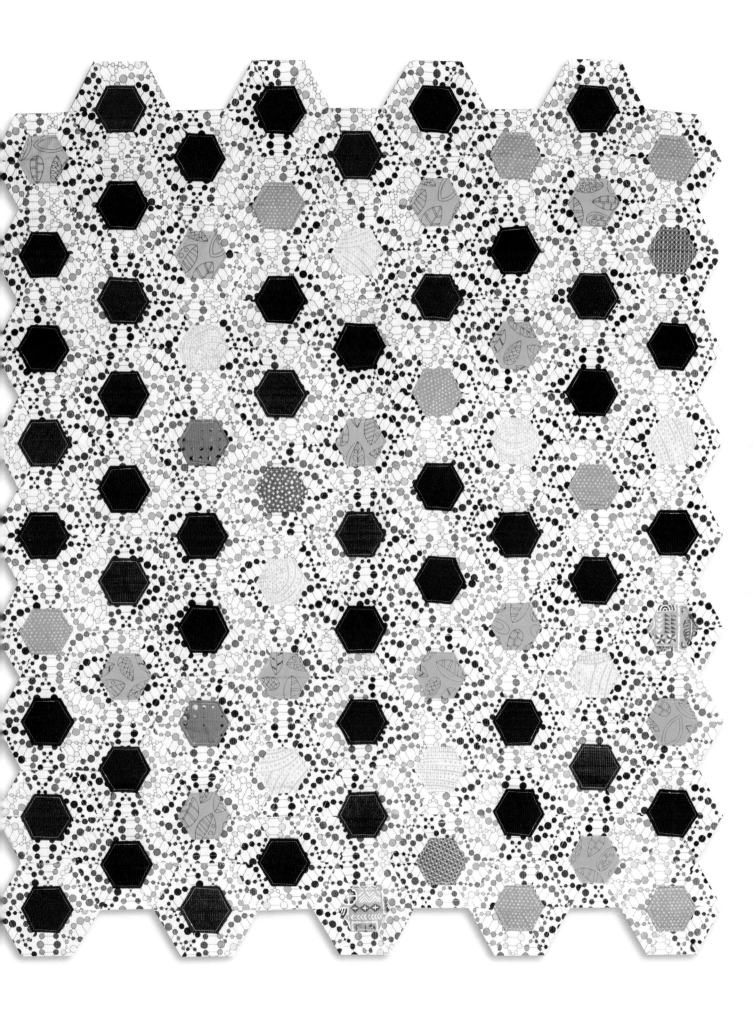

Layout Diagram

Flannel, Plaids, and Solids Baby Quilt

This quilt makes use of 5" (12.7m) and 10" (25.4cm) square precuts, so the project comes together quickly. If you don't have precuts, I've included yardage amounts as well. Don't worry too much about the placement of the FFHs on this project; there's no particular order needed.

Finished size: 49" x 50" (1.68 x 2.16m)

Materials

Note: Fabric requirements are based on 42" (106.7cm) wide fabric. WOF = width of fabric.

- 1½ yards (16.5m) of 90" (2.3m) wide batting
- 110 assorted 10" (25.4m) fabric squares OR 7¾ yards (7.1m) of assorted fabrics
- 110 assorted 5" (12.7cm) fabric squares OR 2 yards (1.83m) of assorted fabrics
- 10" (25.4cm) Circle Template
- 5" (12.7cm) Circle Template
- 5" (12.7cm) Hexagon Template

Cutting

From the batting, cut:

- (8) 6½" (16.5cm) strips of 90" (2.3m) wide batting. From these strips, cut 110 pieces using the 5" (12.7cm) Hexagon Template. Each batting strip yields 15 hexagons

For the bases, cut:

- (110) 10" (25.4cm) circles from the precut squares OR cut (28) 10" (25.4cm) x WOF strips. From these strips, cut (110) 10" (25.4cm) circles. Each strip yields 4 circles

For the toppers, cut:

- (110) 5" (12.7cm) circles from the precut squares OR cut (14) 5" (12.7cm) x WOF strips. From these strips, cut (110) 5" (12.7cm) circles. Each strip yields 8 circles

Instructions

1. Make the FFHs. Following the instructions on page 11, make 110 FFHs, using random combinations of bases and toppers.

2. Lay out the columns. Arrange the FFHs in columns of 10, as shown in the Layout Diagram. Keep the lengthwise straight of grain for each base hexagon oriented the same way (page 19). Sew the FFHs in each column together, starting at the top of the column and working your way down (page 18). Continue until you have 10 columns.

3. Join the columns. Sew column 2 to column 1 using your selected joining stitch. Note that column 1 is taller than column 2. Then attach column 3 to column 2. Next, sew columns 4 and 5 together, and continue to sew adjacent pairs together (6/7, 8/9, 10/11).

Working from left to right, join all units together.

Layout Diagram

Intersecting Shapes Quilt

Saturated colors against a light background create the appearance of intersecting hexagon rings in this lap or wall quilt. Use dark teal for the two smaller hexagon rings and bright orange for the large hexagon ring. The background is made up of assorted fabrics.

Finished size: 55" x 65" (1.4 x 1.65m)

Materials

Note: Fabric requirements are based on 42" (106.7cm) wide fabric. WOF = width of fabric.

- 2 yards (1.83m) of 90" (2.3m) wide batting
- 11 yards (10.06m) assorted light background fabrics
- 2 yards (1.83m) assorted orange fabrics
- 2¼ yards (2.06m) assorted teal fabrics
- 10" (25.4cm) Circle Template
- 5" (12.7cm) Circle Template
- 5" (12.7cm) Hexagon Template

Cutting

From the batting, cut:
- (11) 6½" (16.5cm) strips of 90" (2.3m) wide batting. From these strips, cut 162 pieces using the 5" (12.7cm) Hexagon Template. Each batting strip yields 15 hexagons

From the background fabrics, cut:
- (30) 10" (25.4cm) x WOF strips. From these strips, cut (120) 10" (25.4cm) circles. Each strip yields 4 circles
- (15) 5" (12.7cm) x WOF strips. From these strips, cut (120) 5" (12.7cm) circles. Each strip yields 8 circles

From the orange fabrics, cut:
- (5) 10" (25.4cm) x WOF strips. From these strips, cut (20) 10" (25.4cm) circles. Each strip yields 4 circles
- (3) 5" (12.7cm) x WOF strips. From these strips, cut (20) 5" (12.7cm) circles. Each strip yields 8 circles

From the teal fabrics, cut:
- (6) 10" (25.4cm) x WOF strips. From these strips, cut (22) 10" (25.4cm) circles. Each strip yields 4 circles
- (3) 5" (12.7cm) x WOF strips. From these strips, cut (22) 5" (12.7cm) circles. Each strip yields 8 circles

Instructions

1. Make the FFHs. Following the instructions on page 11, make 120 background FFHs, 20 orange FFHs, and 22 dark teal FFHs (162 FFHs total).

2. Lay out the columns. Arrange the FFHs in alternating columns of 12 and 13, as shown in the Layout Diagram. Keep the lengthwise straight of grain for each base hexagon oriented the same way (page 19), and pin a label on each column to help keep yourself organized. Sew the FFHs in each column together, starting at the top of the column and working your way down (page 18). Continue until you have 13 columns.

3. Join the columns. Sew column 2 to column 1 using your selected joining stitch. Note that column 1 is below column 2. Then attach column 3 to column 2. Next, sew columns 4 and 5 together, and continue to sew adjacent pairs together (6/7, 8/9, 10/11, 12/13).

Working from left to right, join all units together.

Layout Diagram

Hexie Spiral Quilt

The Hexie Spiral Quilt is striking, whether placed on a wall or a twin-size bed. This quilt uses FFHs made from a variety of dark black and red prints against a relatively light background. Make sure there is high contrast between the values (lightness and darkness) of your background and spiral fabrics.

Finished size: 66" x 85" (1.7 x 2.2m)

Materials

Note: Fabric requirements are based on 42" (106.7cm) wide fabric. WOF = width of fabric.

- 3⅛ yards (2.8m) of 90" (2.3m) wide batting
- 12⅓ yards (3.8m) of assorted black on white print fabrics (for the background)
- 10½ yards (9.3m) assorted red print and black print fabrics (for the spiral)
- 10" (25.4cm) Circle Template
- 5" (12.7cm) Circle Template
- 5" (12.7cm) Hexagon Template

Cutting

From the batting, cut:
- (17) 6½" (16.5cm) strips of 90" (2.3m) wide batting. From these strips, cut 255 pieces using the 5" (12.7cm) Hexagon Template. Each batting strip yields 15 hexagons

From the black on white prints, cut:
- (35) 10" (25.4cm) x WOF strips. From these strips, cut (140) 10" (25.4cm) circles. Each strip yields 4 circles
- (18) 5" (12.7cm) x WOF strips. From these strips, cut (140) 5" (12.7cm) circles. Each strip yields 8 circles

From the red prints and black prints, cut:
- (29) 10" (25.4cm) x WOF strips. From these strips, cut (115) 10" (25.4cm) circles. Each strip yields 4 circles
- (15) 5" (12.7cm) x WOF strips. From these strips, cut (115) 5" (12.7cm) circles. Each strip yields 8 circles

Instructions

1. Make the FFHs. Following the instructions on page 11, make 140 FFHs from the black on white fabrics (for the background) and 115 FFHs from the red prints and black prints (for the spiral), for 255 FFHs total.

2. Lay out the columns. Arrange the FFHs as shown in the Layout Diagram, laying out the hexies in columns. Keep the lengthwise straight of grain for each base hexagon oriented the same way (page 19). Label the columns to keep them

organized, then sew the FFHs in each column together, following the instructions on page 1.

3. Join the columns. Sew column 2 to column 1 using your selected joining stitch. Note that column 1 is lower than column 2. Then attach column 3 to column 2. Next, sew columns 4 and 5 together, and continue to sew adjacent pairs together (6/7, 8/9, 10/11, 12/13, 14/15).

Working from left to right, join all units together.

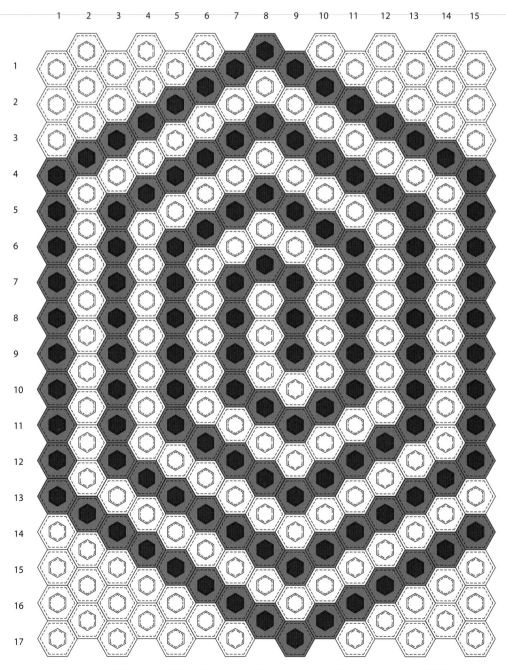

Layout Diagram: The dark spiral is made up of red and black FFHs.

Pathways Quilt

This hexie quilt is made using a variety of relatively bright fabrics against a background of assorted light fabric FFHs. For many sections, I used fabrics of similar a color and value instead of a single fabric. The materials requirements are provided as if a single fabric was used for the whole section.

Finished Size: 66" x 80" (1.7 x 2m)

Materials

Note: Fabric requirements are based on 42" (106.7cm) wide fabric. WOF = width of fabric.

- 3½ yards (3m) of 90" (2.3m) wide batting
- 13¼ yards (11.9m) assorted light background fabrics
- ⅜ yard (34.3cm) assorted light blue fabrics (fabric A)
- 1⅛ yards (1m) assorted light green fabrics (fabric B)
- 1½ yards (1.4m) assorted turquoise fabrics (fabric C)
- 1⅛ yards (1m) assorted orange fabrics (fabric D)
- 1⅞ yards (1.7m) assorted gold fabrics (fabric E)
- 1½ yards (1.4m) assorted multicolored fabrics (fabric F)
- 1¼ yards (1.1m) assorted lime green fabrics (fabric G)
- ⅜ yard (34.3cm) assorted royal blue fabrics (fabric H)
- 10" (25.4cm) Circle Template
- 5" (12.7cm) Circle Template
- 5" (12.7cm) Hexagon Template

Cutting

From the batting, cut:
- (16) 6½" (16.5cm) strips of 90" (2.3m) wide batting. From these strips, cut 256 pieces using the 5" (12.7cm) Hexagon Template. Each batting strip yields 15 hexagons

From the background fabrics, cut:
- (38) 10" (25.4cm) x WOF strips. From these strips, cut (149) 10" (25.4cm) circles. Each strip yields 4 circles
- (19) 5" (12.7cm) x WOF strips. From these strips, cut (149) 5" (12.7cm) circles. Each strip yields 8 circles

From fabric A, cut:
- (2) 10" (25.4cm) x WOF strips. From these strips, cut (2) 10" (25.4cm) circle and (1) 5" (12.7cm) circle

From fabric B, cut:
- (3) 10" (25.4cm) x WOF strips. From these strips, cut (12) 10" (25.4cm) circles. Each strip yields 4 circles
- (2) 5" (12.7cm) x WOF strips. From these strips, cut (12) 5" (12.7cm) circles. Each strip yields 8 circles

From fabric C, cut:
- (4) 10" (25.4cm) x WOF strips. From these strips, cut (15) 10" (25.4cm) circles. Each strip yields 4 circles
- (2) 5" (12.7cm) x WOF strips. From these strips, cut (15) 5" (12.7cm) circles. Each strip yields 8 circles

From fabric D, cut:
- (3) 10" (25.4cm) x WOF strips. From these strips, cut (11) 10" (25.4cm) circles. Each strip yields 4 circles
- (2) 5" (12.7cm) x WOF strips. From these strips, cut (11) 5" (12.7cm) circles. Each strip yields 8 circles

From fabric E, cut:
- (5) 10" (25.4cm) x WOF strips. From these strips, cut (20) 10" (25.4cm) circles. Each strip yields 4 circles
- (3) 5" (12.7cm) x WOF strips. From these strips, cut (20) 5" (12.7cm) circles. Each strip yields 8 circles

From fabric F, cut:
- (4) 10" (25.4cm) x WOF strips. From these strips, cut (16) 10" (25.4cm) circles. Each strip yields 4 circles
- (2) 5" (12.7cm) x WOF strips. From these strips, cut (16) 5" (12.7cm) circles. Each strip yields 8 circles

From fabric G, cut:
- (3) 10" (25.4cm) x WOF strips. From these strips, cut (12) 10" (25.4cm) circles. Each strip yields 4 circles
- (2) 5" (12.7cm) x WOF strips. From these strips, cut (12) 5" (12.7cm) circles. Each strip yields 8 circles

From fabric H, cut:
- (1) 10" (25.4cm) x WOF strips. From this strip, cut (3) 10" (25.4cm) circle and (3) 5" (12.7cm) circles

Instructions

1. Make the FFHs. Following the instructions on page 11, make the following FFHs (240 FFHs total):

✳ 149 FFHs in background fabric
✳ 2 FFHs in fabric A
✳ 12 FFHs in fabric B
✳ 15 FFHs in fabric C
✳ 11 FFHs in fabric D
✳ 20 FFHs in fabric E
✳ 16 FFHs in fabric F
✳ 12 FFHs in fabric G
✳ 3 FFHs in fabric H

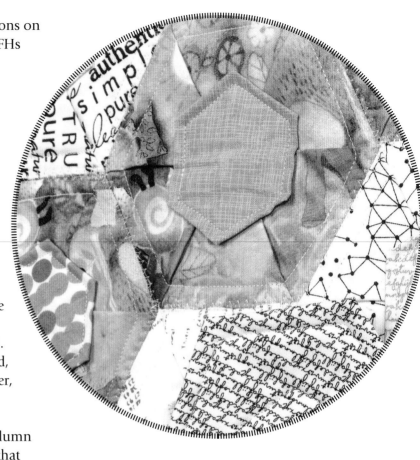

2. Lay out the columns. Arrange the FFHs as shown in the Layout Diagram, laying out the hexies in columns. Keep the lengthwise straight of grain for each base hexagon oriented the same way (page 19). Label the columns to keep them organized, then sew the FFHs in each column together, following the instructions on page 18.

3. Join the columns. Sew column 2 to column 1 using your selected joining stitch. Note that column 1 is higher than column 2. Then attach column 3 to column 2. Next, sew columns 4 and 5 together, and continue to sew adjacent pairs together (6/7, 8/9, 10/11, 12/14, and 14/15).

Working from left to right, join all units together.

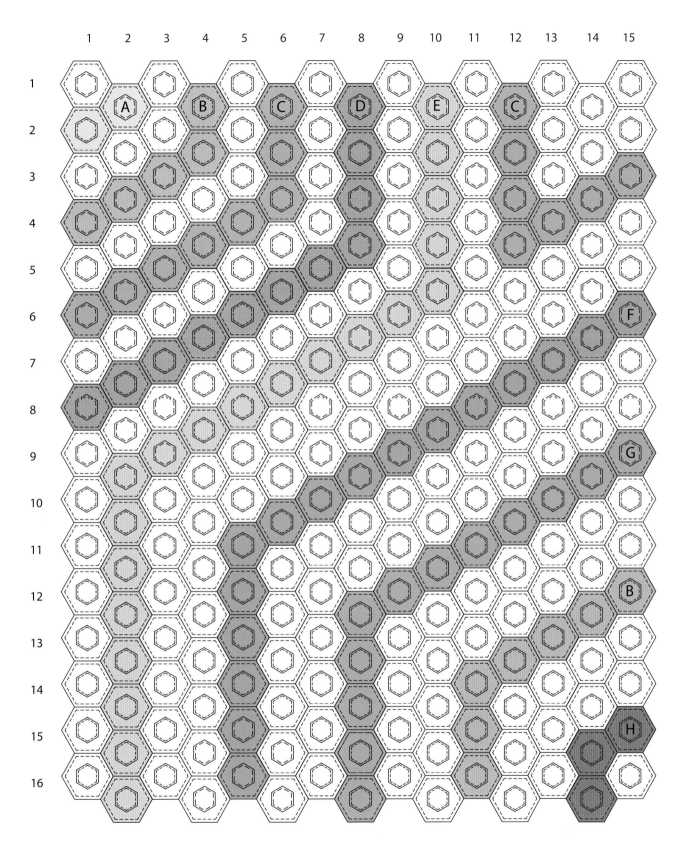

Layout Diagram

Going in Circles Quilt

This quilt is reminiscent of a traditional Around the World quilt, but it uses hexagons instead of squares. You will use one color for the center and then add other rounds of color. Additional hexagon units fill out the corners of the quilt.

Finished size: 91" x 95" (2.3 x 2.4m)

Materials

Note: Fabric requirements are based on 42" (106.7cm) wide fabric. WOF = width of fabric.

- 4⅜ yards (4m) of 90" (2.3m) wide batting
- ⅝ yard (57.2cm) green print fabric (fabric A)
- 1⅛ yards (1m) assorted navy fabrics (fabric B)
- 1⅞ yards (1.7m) assorted green fabrics (fabric C)
- 2⅜ yards (2.2m) assorted blue and yellow fabrics (fabric D)
- 2⅞ yards (2.63m) assorted white fabrics (fabric E)
- 3⅜ yards (3.1m) assorted light green fabrics (fabric F)
- 4 yards (3.7m) assorted yellow fabrics (fabric G)
- 4 yards (3.7m) assorted turquoise fabrics (fabric H)
- 3¾ yards (3.4m) assorted mottled green fabrics (fabric I)
- 7½ yards (6.9m) assorted dark teal fabrics (fabric J)
- 10" (25.4cm) Circle Template
- 5" (12.7cm) Circle Template
- 5" (12.7cm) Hexagon Template

Fabric Note

To give the quilt a scrappier look, mix and match fabrics from different rounds for the toppers. Mix in a few scraps from other prints, solids, and blenders in the same color family.

Cutting

From the batting, cut:
- (24) 6½" (16.5cm) strips of 90" (2.3m) wide batting. From these strips, cut 351 pieces using the 5" (12.7cm) Hexagon Template. Each batting strip yields 15 hexagons

From fabric A, cut:
- (2) 10" (25.4cm) x WOF strips. From these strips, cut (5) 10" (25.4cm) circles. Each strip yields 4 circles
- Cut (5) 5" (12.7cm) circles from the remaining fabric

From fabric B, cut:
- (4) 10" (25.4cm) x WOF strips. From these strips, cut (14) 10" (25.4cm) circles and (14) 5" (12.7cm) circles

From fabric C, cut:
- (5) 10" (25.4cm) x WOF strips. From these strips, cut (20) 10" (25.4cm) circles. Each strip yields 4 circles
- (3) 5" (12.7cm) x WOF strips. From these strips, cut (20) 5" (12.7cm) circles. Each strip yields 8 circles

From fabric D, cut:
- (7) 10" (25.4cm) x WOF strips. From these strips, cut (26) 10" (25.4cm) circles. Each strip yields 4 circles. From the rest of the last strip, also cut (2) 5" (12.7cm) circles
- (3) 5" (12.7cm) x WOF strips. From these strips, cut (24) 5" (12.7cm) circles. Each strip yields 8 circles

From fabric E, cut:
- (8) 10" (25.4cm) x WOF strips. From these strips, cut (32) 10" (25.4cm) circles. Each strip yields 4 circles
- (4) 5" (12.7cm) x WOF strips. From these strips, cut (32) 5" (12.7cm) circles. Each strip yields 8 circles

From fabric F, cut:

- (10) 10" (25.4cm) x WOF strips. From these strips, cut (38) 10" (25.4cm) circles. Each strip yields 4 circles. From the rest of the last strip, also cut (6) 5" (12.7cm) circles
- (4) 5" (12.7cm) x WOF strips. From these strips, cut (32) 5" (12.7cm) circles. Each strip yields 8 circles

From fabric G, cut:

- (11) 10" (25.4cm) x WOF strips. From these strips, cut (44) 10" (25.4cm) circles. Each strip yields 4 circles
- (6) 5" (12.7cm) x WOF strips. From these strips, cut (44) 5" (12.7cm) circles. Each strip yields 8 circles

From fabric H, cut:

- (11) 10" (25.4cm) x WOF strips. From these strips, cut (44) 10" (25.4cm) circles. Each strip yields 4 circles
- (6) 5" (12.7cm) x WOF strips. From these strips, cut (44) 5" (12.7cm) circles. Each strip yields 8 circles

From fabric I, cut:

- (11) 10" (25.4cm) x WOF strips. From these strips, cut (42) 10" (25.4cm) circles. Each strip yields 4 circles
- (5) 5" (12.7cm) x WOF strips. From these strips, cut (42) 5" (12.7cm) circles. Each strip yields 8 circles

From fabric J, cut:

- (22) 10" (25.4cm) x WOF strips. From these strips, cut (86) 10" (25.4cm) circles. From the last strip, also cut (6) 5" (12.7cm) circles. Each strip yields 4 circles
- (10) 5" (12.7cm) x WOF strips. From these strips, cut (80) 5" (12.7cm) circles. Each strip yields 8 circles

Instructions

1. Make the FFHs. Following the instructions on page 11, prepare the following FFHs (307 FFHs total):

- ✳ 5 FFHs in fabric A
- ✳ 14 FFHs in fabric B
- ✳ 20 FFHs in fabric C
- ✳ 26 FFHs in fabric D
- ✳ 32 FFHs in fabric E
- ✳ 38 FFHs in fabric F
- ✳ 44 FFHs in fabric G
- ✳ 44 FFHs in fabric H
- ✳ 42 FFHs in fabric I
- ✳ 86 FFHs in fabric J

2. Lay out the columns. Arrange the FFHs as shown in the Layout Diagram, laying out the hexies in columns. Keep the lengthwise straight of grain for each base hexagon oriented the same way (page 19). Each column has either 18 or 19 FFHs. Label the columns to keep them organized, then sew the FFHs in each column together, following the instructions on page 18.

3. Join the columns. Sew column 2 to column 1 using your selected joining stitch. Note that column 1 is higher than column 2. Then attach column 3 to column 2. Next, sew columns 4 and 5 together, and continue to sew adjacent pairs together (6/7, 8/9, 10/11, 12/13, 14/15, 16/17, 18/19).

Working from left to right, join all units together.

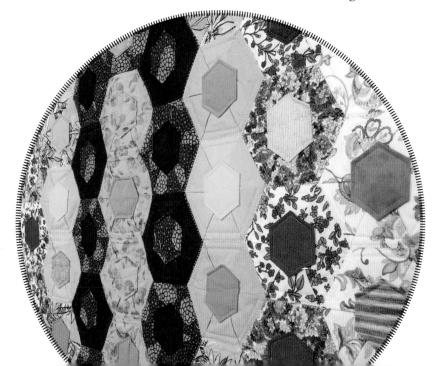

Layout Diagram

Anything Goes Scrap Quilt

The name "Anything Goes" refers to the fact that nearly anything and everything in my stash made its way into the quilt. Nearly every color is represented, ranging from light to dark. Aside from the border, I made no more than two 5" (12.7cm) bases of any one fabric. This quilt contains nearly 1,500 FFHs, and it is constructed a little differently than others in this book.

Finished size: 83" x 95" (1.7 x 2.2m)

Materials

Note: Fabric requirements are based on 42" (106.7cm) wide fabric. WOF = width of fabric.

- 5⅜ yards (4.92m) of 90" (2.3m) wide batting
- 23 yards (21m) total of assorted fabrics OR (32) 40-count 5" (12.7cm) square charm packs (for center hexie bases)
- 5¾ yards (5.3m) total assorted fabrics OR (32) 40-count 2½" (6.4cm) square charm packs (for center hexie toppers)
- 5 yards (4.6m) blender fabric for border
- 5" (12.7cm) Circle Template
- 2½" (6.4cm) Circle Template
- 2½" (6.4cm) Hexagon Template

Cutting

From the batting, cut:

- (55) 3½" (8.9cm) strips of 90" (2.3m) wide batting. From these strips, cut 1,482 pieces using the 2½" (6.4cm) Hexagon Template. Each batting strip yields 27 hexagons

For the center hexie bases, cut:

- Cut (158) 5" (12.7cm) x WOF strips. From these strips, cut (1,258) 5" (12.7cm) circles. Each strip yields 8 circles. If using precuts, there's no need to cut into strips first.

For the center hexie toppers, cut:

- Cut (79) 2½" (6.4cm) x WOF strips. From these strips, cut (1,258) 2½" (6.4cm) circles. Each strip yields 16 circles. If using precuts, there's no need to cut into strips first.

From the border fabric, cut:

- Cut (28) 5" (12.7cm) x WOF strips. From these strips, cut (224) 5" (12.7cm) circles. Each strip yields 8 circles
- Cut (28) 2½" (6.4cm) x WOF strips. From these strips, cut (224) 2½" (6.4cm) circles. Each strip yields 16 circles

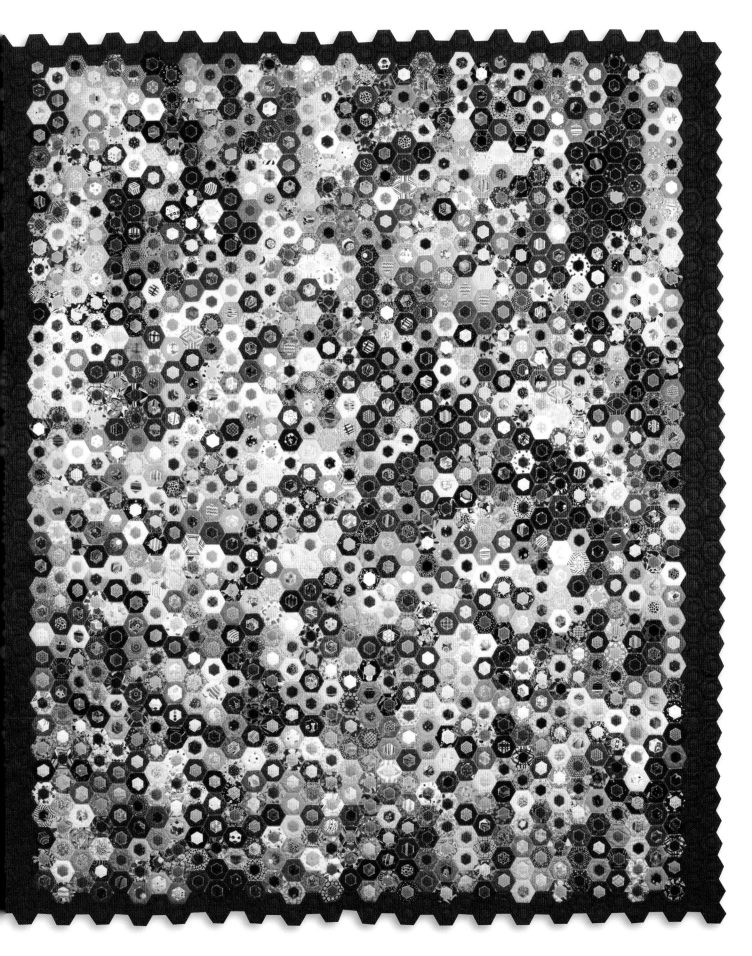

Instructions

1. Make the FFHs. Following the instructions on page 11, make 1,258 FFHs from center base and center topper fabric, and 224 FFHs from the border fabric, for 1,482 FFHs total.

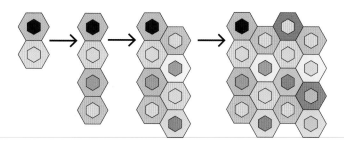

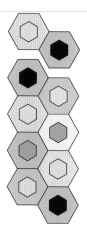

A four-FFH unit and a sixteen-FFH unit.

2. Build FFH units. Due to the size of this quilt, the quilt starts by building small units of FFHs and gradually joining them into larger units. Start by combining FFHs into units of 2, then join those into columns of 4, join columns of 4 into columns of 8, and finally join columns of 8 into columns of 16. For instructions on joining FFHs, see page 14.

You need: (72) 16-FFH units, (9) 8-FFH units, (1) 2-FFH unit, and (8) 4-FFH units, as shown.

A two-FFH unit and an eight-FFH unit.

Tips for Making This Quilt

The size of this quilt and the number of FFHs required make this project more of an undertaking than the other projects in this book. Here are some tips from my experience making the quilt:

- **Use your stash:** I combed through my stash and cut chunks of fabric large enough for the 5" or 2½" circles. I also used 5" square charm packs and a set of 2½" x WOF strips of solid fabrics.
- **Cut in batches:** I worked in batches cutting large circles, small circles, and batting pieces. Once I had plenty of circles to choose from, about 50–100, I carefully chose large and small circle pairs that looked great together and stacked them with a piece of batting so they would be ready for folding and pinning. I like to think of each FFH as a small work of art.
- **Sew in batches:** Periodically, I spent time folding, inserting batting, and pinning the FFH, completing about 15 to 20 at a time. Then, I sewed the toppers to the hexie bases using a buttonhole stitch to make FFH units. I set finished FFHs aside until there were plenty before making larger groups of FFHs.
- **Group color friends:** When making the 16-unit columns, I looked for some colors that blended or looked really good near each other. I believe this created some color coherence in a project that has so many different fabrics and colors.
- **Keep thread simple:** Because of the multiple colors used in this quilt, I simply used white thread for all sewing in the center of the quilt. For the border, a rust colored thread was used.

Top and Bottom Border; make 2.

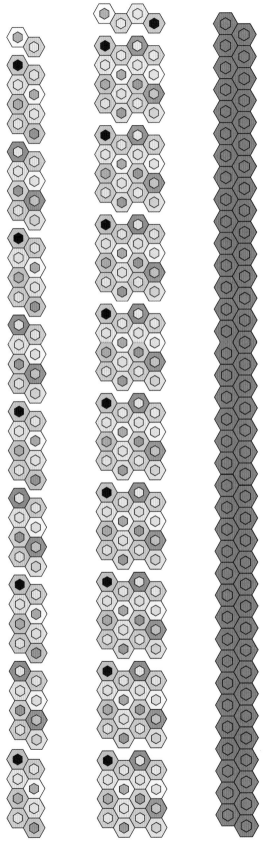

Column 1   Columns 2–9   Side Border;
                                        make 2

3. Sew the columns. Arrange the (9) 8-FFH units together in the order desired for the first column and add a 2-FFH unit at the top, as shown. This is column 1.

Arrange columns 2 through 9 as shown, using (9) 16-FFH units and (1) 4-FFH unit per column, as shown. Pin a column number to the top of each column to keep the columns organized.

Keep the lengthwise straight of grain for each base hexagon oriented in the same direction, (page 19). Starting at the top of the column 1, sew the FFH units together, and continue to sew the units in each individual column, until you have 9 complete columns.

4. Make the borders. Make 2 sets of 2 columns with 37 FFH for the side borders. Sew 2 columns together for the left border and 2 columns together for the right border.

Make 2 sets of 2 columns with 38 FFHs for the top and bottom borders, as shown.

5. Join the quilt. Sew the left border to column 1 (each only 2 FFHs wide). Then add column 2 to the left border/column 1 unit. Add column 3 to column 2 and continue until column 9 is joined. Sew the right border to column 9. Add the top border, then the bottom border.

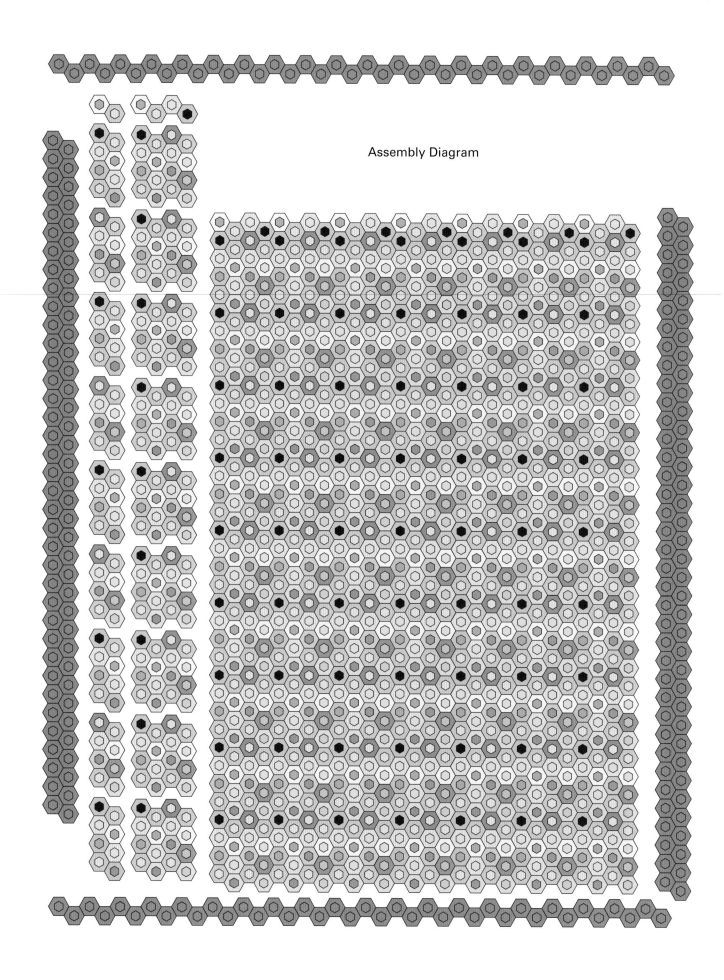

Assembly Diagram

Homage to the Hexagon Quilt

If one hexie topper is good, more is better! For this lap quilt, multiple toppers are stacked onto a hexie base; I call this technique stacked FFHs. The project is called Homage to the Hexagon as a nod to the work of Josef Albers, Homage to the Square. After making the stacked FFHs, I sewed them together by hand. Varying the color, value, and size of the toppers helps move the eye around the quilt.

Finished size: 63" x 56" (1.6 x 1.4m)

Materials

Note: Because of the varying number of toppers, the fabric amounts are estimates. About 2 fat quarters for each FFH should provide plenty of fabric.

- 98 fat quarters or equivalent amount of fabric
- 1⅞ yards (171.5cm) of 90" (2.3m) wide batting
- 18" (45.7cm) Circle Template
- 15" (38.1cm) Circle Template
- 12" (30.5cm) Circle Template
- 9" (22.9cm) Circle Template
- 6" (15.2cm) Circle Template
- 3" (7.6cm) Circle Template
- 9" (22.9cm) Hexagon Template

Cutting

From the batting, cut:
- (6) 11¼" (28.4cm) strips of 90" (2.3m) wide batting. From these strips, cut 49 pieces using the 9" (22.9cm) Hexagon Template. Each batting strip yields 9 hexagons

From the fat quarters, cut:
- (49) 18" (45.7) circles for the bases
- Assorted 15" (38.1cm), 12" (30.5cm), 9" (22.9cm), 6" (15.2cm), and 3" (7.6cm) circles for the toppers

Cutting Tip

I found it most convenient to cut large circles one at a time using a quarter-circle template with folded fabric.

1. Lay out the stacks. Select an 18" (45.7cm) circle for your base and several smaller circles for the tops. Lay out each grouping before you start sewing.

2. Make the FFHs. Select an FFH base. Add batting, fold, and pin (page 11). Fold the other selected topper circles without batting.

Begin sewing the layers from the top down, sewing your smallest topper to the next largest topper. Align the hexies with the folds, not the points, and keep the straight of grain the same direction (page 19). Except for the topmost FFH, the folds should face up.

Construction Tip

I find it helpful to fold and pin a group of hexies before sewing. I use safety pins to hold the groupings together until sewing. Look for opportunities to batch your sewing so you don't have to rethread your machine as often. Skipped stitches usually indicate a problem with the needle; either a new needle is needed or the needle is not right for the job. I used a denim needle (also called jeans needle), size 16 or 18, because of the multiple layers.

Sew the smallest topper, with the folds facing down, to the second smallest topper.

Sew the completed topper unit to the base.

Sew the topper unit to the next layer, and finally sew the completed topper unit to the base. Finally, sew around the outer edge of the base FFH. Repeat this process with each stack of hexies, completing 49 FFHs.

3. Lay out the columns. Arrange the FFHs as desired into 7 columns with 7 FFHs each. Keep the lengthwise straight of grain for each base hexagon oriented in the same direction (page 19). Label your columns, then sew the hexies together in each column, starting at the top and working your way down.

4. Join the columns. Sew column 2 to column 1 using your selected joining stitch. Note that column 1 is lower than column 2. Next, join column 3, to columns 1/2, then join column 4, and continue until all columns are sewn together.

Layout Diagram
Your colors will vary based on your own fabrics.

Flower Wall Hanging

FFHs can be used for a variety of techniques, including appliqué. Because FFHs have finished edges, there is no fiddly turning of the edges before appliquéing. In this wall hanging, FFHs are made into flowers, which are then added to a background fabric. The whole project comes together quickly.

Finished size: 35" x 41" (0.9 x 1m)

Materials

Note: Fabric requirements are based on 42" (106.7cm) wide fabric. WOF = width of fabric.

- 41" (1.5m) x 47" (1.2m) piece or 1¼ yards (1.1m) of 90" (2.3m) wide batting , plus optional scrap batting for flowers
- 1¼ yards (1.14m) background fabric
- 1¼ yards (1.14m) backing fabric
- ¾ yard (68.6cm) fabric for stems, leaves, and binding
- 3 fat quarters in desired colors for flowers (1 fat quarter is enough for each flower; alternatively, use ¼ yard [22.9cm] of fabric or scraps for each flower)
- 6" (15.2cm) Circle Template
- 3" (7.6cm) Circle Template
- 3" (7.6cm) Hexagon Template (optional)

Materials Note

Batting is optional for the FFHs in this project; it will make the flowers more dimensional, but it is not necessary. The wall hanging shown here uses batting.

Cutting Instructions

From the batting scraps, cut (optional):
- 25 pieces using the 3" (7.6cm) Hexagon Template

For each flower, cut:
- (7) 6" (15.2cm) circles
- (7) 3" (7.6cm) circles

From the stem, leaf, and binding fabric, cut:
- (4) 6" (15.2cm) circles
- (4) 3" (7.6cm) circles
- (4) 2½" (6.4cm) x WOF strips (for binding)

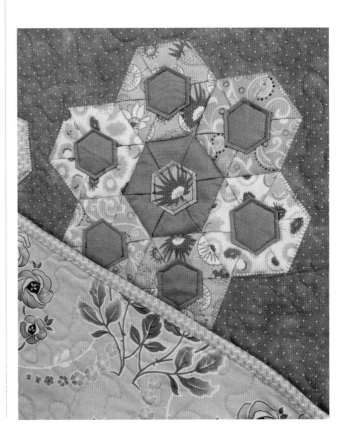

Instructions

1. Make the FFHs. Following the instructions on page 11, make 7 FFHs for each flower, and 4 FFHs for the leaves; 25 FFHs total. Do not sew around the outer edge of the hexie base after joining the topper; the edges will get sewn when the pieces are appliquéd.

2. Join the flowers. Arrange the 7 FFHs for each flower, then sew each flower together using the method described on page 16. Add the center hexies last. I sewed mine together by hand.

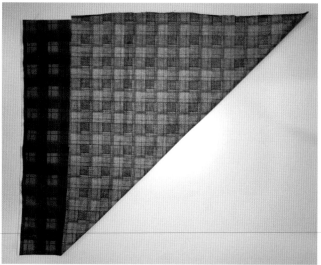

3. Cut the bias strips. Fold a piece of stem fabric as shown to find the 45-degree angle. Cut the fold with a scissors or cut the fold off with a rotary cutter and ruler.

Cut 1¼" (3.2cm) wide strips from the bias edge of the fabric and sew them together on the diagonal until the strip is long enough. The total finished stem lengths are about 26" (66cm), 25" (64cm), and 23" (58.4cm). Make the stems at least 3" (7.6cm) longer than the finished size.

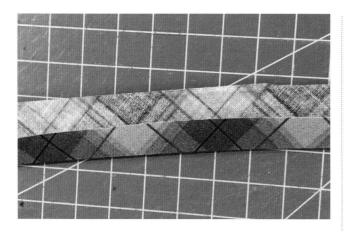

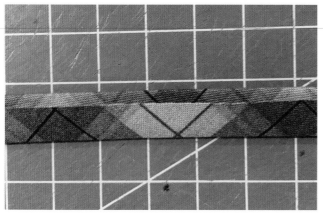

5. Appliqué the flowers, leaves, and stems.
Arrange the flowers on the background as desired. Place and pin the bias flower stems, tucking one end of a stem under a flower. Stitch in the ditch around the center hexies of each flower to anchor them to the background.

Sew around each flower using a buttonhole stitch, or other chosen stitch, then sew the bias stems in place by sewing close to each edge with a straight stitch.

Position and pin the leaves. Appliqué into place with a buttonhole stitch.

6. Finish the quilt. Layer the backing, batting, and quilt top together and baste. Quilt as desired.

Sew the binding strips together on the diagonal to make one long strip. Press with the wrong sides together to make one long folded strip. Sew to the quilt top, matching up the raw edges with the edge of the quilt and folding at the corners to create mitered binding corners. Sew by hand to the other side.

4. Make the bias tape. Working on the wrong side, fold about one-third of the bias strip towards the center. Press well. Then fold from the other side so that the raw edge is just short of the opposite fold. Press well. This makes a bias strip that can be curved for the stems of the flowers.

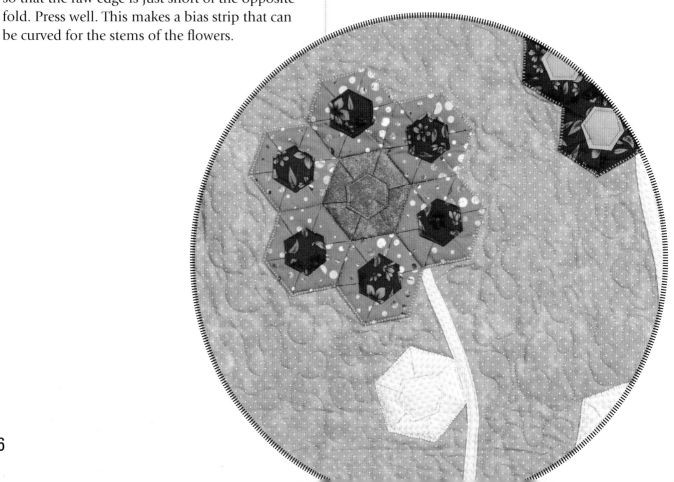

Floating Hexagons Quilt

Each floating hexagon block starts with a small hexagon, and you then add strings around the hexagon. Strings are irregular strips of fabric, varying in width and shape. The string hexagons are appliquéd into place and seem to float on the background. The outside border includes appliquéd FFH base pieces turned upside down.

Finished size: 60" x 70" (1.5 x 1.8m)

Materials

Note: Fabric requirements are based on 42" (106.7cm) wide fabric. WOF = width of fabric.

- 2 yards (1.8m) 90" (2.3m) wide batting
- 5 yards (4.6m) 20" (50.8cm) wide lightweight fusible interfacing, such as Pellon® P44F
- 3 yards (2.7m) light background fabric
- 3 yards (2.7m) total of assorted black, red, white on black, and gray prints
- ¼ yard (22.9cm) total of assorted black prints for first border
- 1 yard (91.4cm) red blender fabric for second border
- ½ yard (45.7cm) binding fabric
- 3¾ yards (3.4m) backing fabric
- 3½" (8.9cm) Hexagon Template
- 5" (12.7cm) Circle Template

Cutting Instructions

From the background fabric, cut (optional):
- (4) 15½" (39.4cm) x WOF pieces. From these pieces, cut (8) 15½" (39.4cm) squares. Each strip yields 2 squares
- (2) 20½" (52.1 cm) x WOF pieces. From these pieces, cut (3) 20½" (52.1 cm) squares. Each strip yields 2 squares

From the assorted black, red, white on black, and gray prints, cut:
- Assorted strips of fabric about 1" (2.5cm) to 2" (5cm) wide to use for string hexagons. Include pieces with an angle to add interest.
- (44) 5" (12.7cm) circles for the border hexies

From the assorted black prints, cut:
- (7) 1¾" (4.445cm) x WOF strips for the inner border

From the red blender fabric, cut:
- (7) 5" (12.7cm) x WOF strips for the second border

From the binding fabric, cut:
- (7) 2½" (6.4cm) x WOF strips

From the backing fabric, cut:
- 2 lengthwise pieces, removing the selvage edge. Sew the pieces together.

Design Note

Vary the fabric, color, width, and the angle of strings to add interest to the floating hexagons. Have fun with these.

Instructions

1. Make templates. Use the 3½" (8.9cm) Hexagon Template to cut out a small starter hexagon from fabric.

Cut paper foundations using newsprint or similar. For making string hexagons, use a 12" (30.5cm) square for the 15" (38.1cm) blocks and a 15" (38.1cm) square for the 20" (51cm) blocks. Paper foundations help keep everything flat as you work.

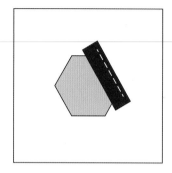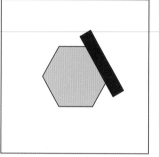
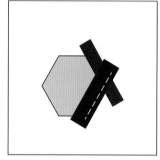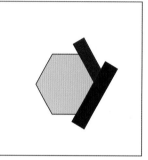

2. Add the strings. Position the small fabric hexagon on the paper foundation and pin it. Place strings right side down on the pinned hexagon, matching the right raw edges. Sew a ¼" (0.64 cm) seam. Open and press. Add another string. Cut off the excess fabric from previous strings with scissors. Open and press.

Continue adding strings clockwise around the center hexagon until the hexagon is as large as you want, but smaller than the foundation square. Trim the hexagon to straighten all the sides.

3. Add the interfacing. Cut a piece of lightweight fusible interfacing larger than the hexagon. Position the interfacing pebbly side up. Place the string hexagon right side down. Sew ¼" (0.6cm) from the edge of the hexagon. Remove the foundation paper.

Cut a slit into the interfacing at about the center of the hexagon. Turn the hexagon right side out, working carefully to prevent tearing the interfacing. Finger-press all around the edges, pinning as needed to keep things in place.

4. Appliqué to the background block. Position the hexagon on the background fabric square. Pin and then press into place. Appliqué to the background using a blind hem stitch, blanket stitch, or other stitch of your choosing.

Remove the excess background fabric and the interfacing through the back of the quilt to reduce bulk in the finished quilt.

Repeat steps 2 to 4 to make (8) 15" (31cm) blocks and (3) 20" (50.8cm) blocks.

5. Join quilt blocks. Lay out the quilt as desired, using the Layout Diagram as a guide. Column 1 has 4 small blocks, column 2 has 3 large blocks, and column 3 has 4 small blocks.

Sew the blocks in each column together using a ¼" (0.6cm) seam and press the seams open. Then sew the 3 columns together using a ¼" (0.6cm) seam. Press the seams.

6. Prepare the borders. Sew the (7) 1¾" (4.5cm) x WOF black fabric strips together into one long strip for the inner borders. Sew the (7) 5" (12.7cm) x WOF red strips together into one long strip for the second borders. Sew the long 1¾" (4.5cm) black strip to one side of the long 5" (12.7cm) red strip. Press the seam. Set aside.

7. Prepare the border hexies. Fold the 5" (12.7cm) circles into hexies (44 total, or desired number); pin the hexies to help them keep their shape as you fold. Note that these hexies do not have batting or toppers. Once folded, spritz with spray starch and press with a flat iron on the flat side of each hexie, removing the pins as you press.

8. Finish the side borders. Measure the quilt from top to bottom. Cut 2 border sections to this size. Arrange the starched and pressed hexagons on the 2 borders as desired and pin; I did not arrange them in exact positions. Machine or hand sew in place, then sew the borders onto the quilt.

9. Finish the top and bottom borders. Measure the quilt from side to side. Cut 2 border sections to this size. Arrange the remaining starched and pressed hexagons on the 2 borders as desired; I did not arrange them in exact positions. Machine or hand sew in place, then sew the borders onto the quilt.

10. Finish the quilt. Layer the backing, batting, and quilt top together and baste. Quilt as desired. Sew the binding strips together on the diagonal to make one long strip. Press with the wrong sides together to make one long folded strip. Sew to the quilt top, matching up the raw edges with the edge of the quilt and folding at the corners to create mitered binding corners. Sew by hand to the other side.

Detail of the quilt border
with appliquéd hexies.

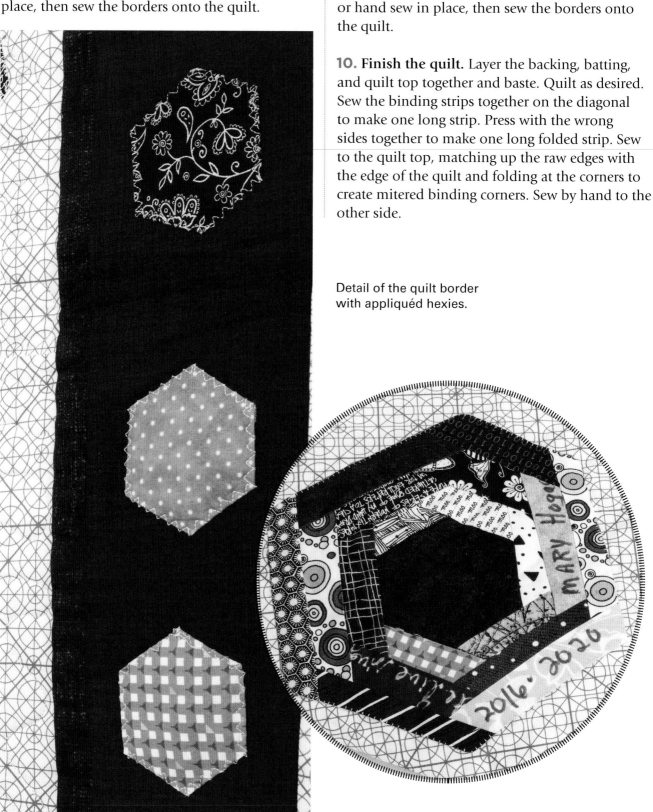

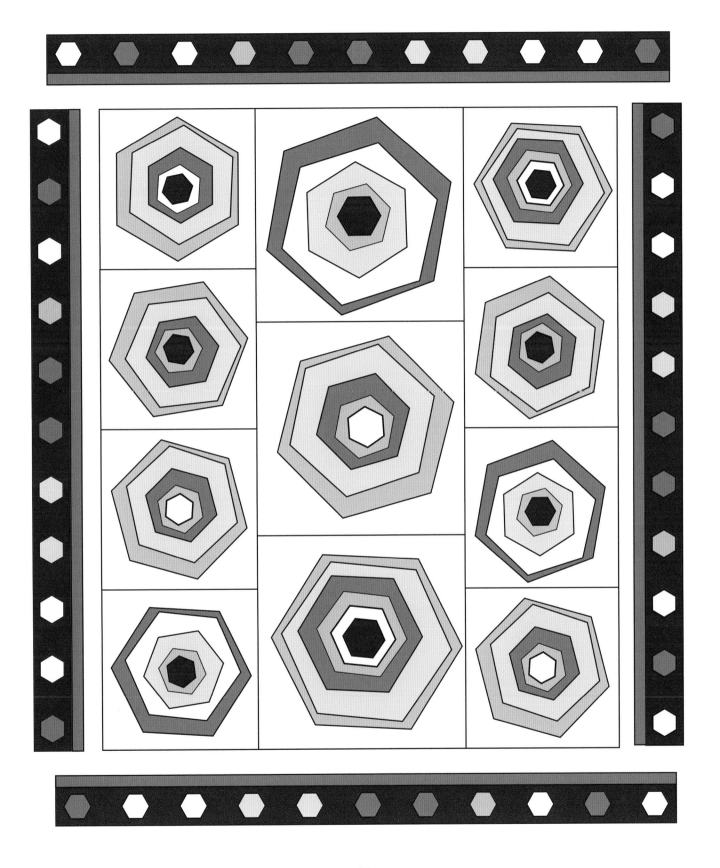

Layout Diagram

Names and Words: Skye's Quilt

I made this quilt for my grandniece for her second birthday, just as she was starting to recognize the letters in her own name. You can use FFH as dots to create any large-scale letters and words. This project shows just one example. Appliqué the FFHs onto a plain background to help the letters pop.

Finished size: 40" x 60" (1.2 x 1.5m)

Materials

Note: Because the number of FFH needed for letters is variable, fabric information for FFHs is not included here. Fabric requirements are based on 42" (106.7cm) wide fabric. WOF = width of fabric.

- 1⅜ yards (1.3m) 90" (2.3m) wide batting; plus additional for FFHs (optional)
- Fabric for FFHs; can be single color or scrappy, precuts, or yardage
- 2 yards (1.8m) background fabric
- 2 yards (1.8m) backing fabric
- ½ yard (45.7cm) binding fabric
- 5" (12.7cm) Circle Template
- 2½" (6.4cm) Circle Template
- 2½" (6.4cm) Hexagon Template

Cutting Instructions

From the batting, cut (optional):
- Needed number of pieces using the 2½" (6.4cm) Hexagon Template

From the FFH fabric, cut:
- Needed number of 5" (12.7cm) circles
- Needed number of 2½" (6.4cm) circles

From the binding fabric, cut:
- (6) 2½" (6.4cm) x WOF strips

Instructions

1. Make the FFHs. Following the instructions on page 11, make the required number of FFHs for your word. Do not sew around the outer edge of the hexie base after joining the topper; the edges will get sewn when the pieces are appliquéd. Batting is optional.

As you start building your letters, it will become clear how many FFHs you need. For reference, the name "Skye" required 37 FFHs.

2. Lay out the FFHs. Arrange the individual FFHs on the background fabric to make letters. Pin and baste into place. If using a sewing machine, use a longer stitch for basting.

3. Appliqué the FFHs. Appliqué each FFH to the background with the desired stitch.

4. Finish the quilt. Layer the backing, batting, and quilt top together and baste. Quilt as desired.

Sew the binding strips together on the diagonal to make one long strip. Press with the wrong sides together to make one long folded strip. Sew to the quilt top, matching up the raw edges with the edge of the quilt and folding at the corners to create mitered binding corners. Sew by hand to the other side.

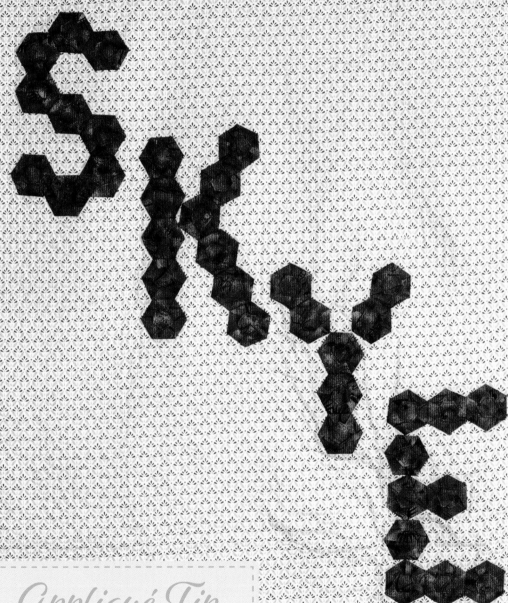

Appliqué Tip

I chose to appliqué my FFHs by hand, to avoid turning the quilt around in the machine. You may also find it easier to appliqué by hand.

Advanced Techniques

Now that you've worked through a few projects and are comfortable with the FFH process, let's look at a few techniques that can take your projects to the next level.

Fussy Cutting

Fussy cutting refers to cutting out and using particular motifs (a distinctive design, pattern, or picture) from fabric. Using this technique with FFHs can provide dramatic results; the toppers are a perfect canvas for fussy-cut designs. The most important thing is to test different options before cutting all your fabric.

HOW TO FUSSY CUT FFHS

✳ Select a possible fussy-cut motif to use for an FFH topper.
✳ Use circle templates about twice the diameter of the fussy-cut design. If desired, cut out a smaller circle from the center of a paper template or mark a center circle on a plastic template so that you can see the motif centered in your circle.
✳ Cut out circles, centering the motif.
✳ Make an FFH topper (do not use batting).
✳ Play with placement and size of toppers and bases to find what you like best.

This table topper uses a 7" (17.8cm) circle for the topper, and 10" (25.4cm) circles for the bases. Because the flower toppers are so close to the edge of the base FFHs, no additional quilting is added to the hexie bases.

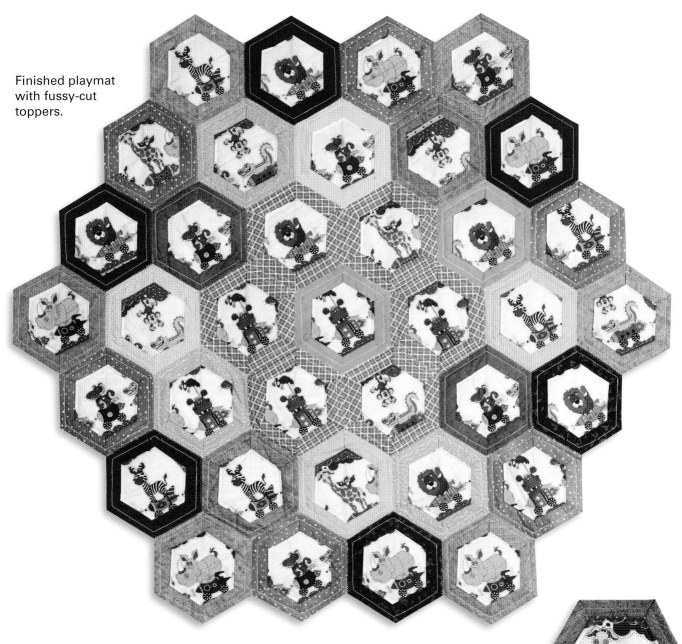

Finished playmat with fussy-cut toppers.

DETERMINING TOPPER SIZE

Sometimes, it's not obvious what size circle to cut for your fussy-cut toppers. For example, this border fabric looked like it would work well for a baby quilt, but the animals themselves varied in size and shape. I needed to experiment to find the right combination of topper size and base hexie. I went with a 10" (25.4cm) topper and 15" (38.1cm) base. The larger topper allowed more of the animal to fit, and the larger base gave the topper more breathing room.

After figuring out the size that looked best to me, I made a baby playmat using 37 FFHs. A center FFH is surrounded by three rounds of hexagons, with alternating base colors on the second and third rounds.

A 10" (25.4cm) topper on a 15" (38.1cm) base (left) is my preferred size for this fabric. The 9" (22.9cm) topper on a 12" (30.5cm) base (top right) and 10" (25.4cm) topper on a 12" (30.5cm) base (lower right) weren't quite right.

MISTAKES HAPPEN

Working with fussy-cut designs can be hit or miss, and I've had my share of misses. I'd like to share a project where things went wrong, so you can learn from my mistakes.

The Fabric

This fabric (from the Kaffe Fassett Collective for Free Spirit) had 4" (10.2cm) squares throughout. I was absolutely sure that I could simply cut 4" (1.02cm) circles out of those squares. I was so wrong.

After folding the 4" (10.2cm) circle cut from a 4" (10.2cm) square, it was clear that my flowers weren't centered the way I'd intended.

Next, I used a 5" (12.7cm) circle, centering it on the 4" (10.2cm) square. This was better, but still a bit off. It was only then that I realized the flower centers were not always at the middle of the 4" (10.2cm) squares. I solved this by using a 5" (12.7cm) circle and centering the circle at the center of each flower. This provides a more symmetric display of the flowers.

Because my final selection of topper was 5" (12.7cm), I decided to use 10" (25.4cm) circles for the hexie bases. I made a large mug mat with a center FFH surrounded by six more FFHs. In retrospect, I think a smaller base would have worked better; the flowers get lost against the background. Remember to test your topper on a base before you cut everything out.

Testing the size and position of fussy cuts. The top examples didn't work; the bottom samples are much better.

Fabric from the Kaffe Fassett Collective for Free Spirit.

Large base hexies make the fussy-cut flowers look lost.

Pieced Fast-Fold Hexies

Trying pieced FFH was a happy accident: A friend wanted to learn to fold FFHs, but having only small scraps at the time, she sewed two pieces together before we folded the hexagon. I became intrigued by the possibilities.

This chapter provides an introduction to two-piece FFHs, four-piece FFHs, and six-piece FFHs. Pieced FFH are folded in the usual way, after making circles from two, four, or six pieces of fabric.

TWO-PIECE FAST-FOLD HEXIES

Two-piece FFHs are made using circles pieced from two rectangles. These instructions will make 10" (25.4cm) bases with 5" (12.7cm) toppers.

1. Make the base. Sew (2) 10" x 5¼" (25.4 x 13.3cm) rectangles together with a ¼" (0.6cm) seam on the long side and press. Cut a 10" (25.4cm) circle, centering the seam across the center of the circle.

2. Make the topper. Sew (2) 5" x 2¾" (12.7 x 7cm) rectangles together with a ¼" (0.6cm) seam on the long side and press. Cut a 5" (12.7cm) circle, centering the seam across the center of the circle.

3. Make the FFH. Fold the FFH base and topper pieces as usual according to the directions on page 11.

Here is the first pieced FFH that I folded.

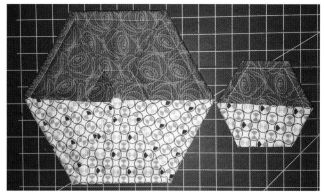

Folding any circle with the seam positioned horizontally will give you the base and topper shown.

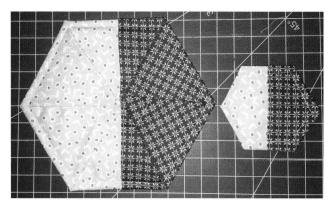

Folding any circle with the seam positioned vertically will give you the base and topper shown.

Combining the finished hexie bases and toppers offers many design possibilities, just a few of which are shown here.

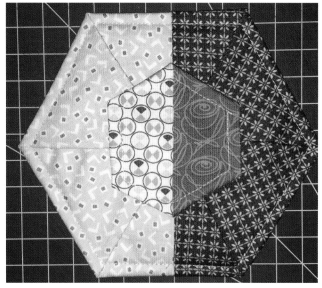

Vertical seam two-piece FFH base with horizontal seam two-piece FFH topper. Remember, the topper is rotated relative to the base to place the points between the folds.

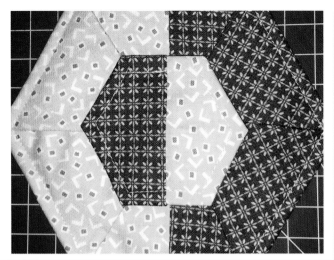

Vertical seam two-piece FFH base with vertical seam two-piece FFH topper.

Horizontal seam two-piece FFH base with horizontal seam two-piece FFH topper.

Horizontal seam two-piece FFH base with vertical seam two-piece FFH topper.

FOUR-PIECE FAST-FOLD HEXIES

Four-piece FFHs are made using circles pieced from four squares of fabric. The instructions below are for just one example of a four-piece FFH.

1. Make the base. Sew (4) 5½" (14cm) squares together into a 4-patch block using ¼" (0.6cm) seams. Press the seams as shown (pressing seams in this way helps when folding). Loosen the threads at the center with a seam ripper if needed so that you can press this flat. Cut a 10" (25.4cm) circle, centering the seams at the center of the circle.

2. Make the topper. Sew (4) 3" (7.6cm) squares together into a 4-patch block using ¼" (0.6cm) seams. Press the seams as shown (pressing seams in this way helps when folding). Loosen the threads at the center with a seam ripper if needed so that you can press this flat. Cut a 5" (12.7cm) circle, centering the seams at the center of the circle.

3. Make the FFH. Fold the FFH base and topper pieces as usual according to the directions on page 11.

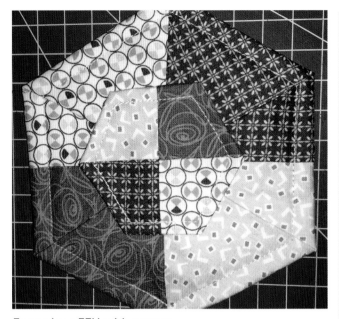

Four-piece FFH with topper.

SIX-PIECE FAST-FOLD HEXIES

Six-Piece FFHs are made using circles pieced from (6) 60-degree triangles. Sewing instructions are for a 10" (25.4cm) base and 5" (12.7cm) base. A 60-degree triangle ruler is needed. Only the base is pieced in this example.

1. Cut the fabric. Cut 6" (15.2cm) wide strips of 3 different fabrics. Layer the fabrics right side up, then cut (2) 60-degree triangles through all 3 fabrics for each FFH.

2. Piece the fabric. Decide on the order and sew 3 segments together with a ¼" (0.6cm) seam allowance. Then sew the other 3 together in the same order. With the points facing up, press the seams to the right. Sew the (2) 3-piece sections together, matching the center point carefully. Press all seams in the same direction, loosening a few threads at the center as needed. The seam allowances form sort of a spiral around the center point.

3. Cut the circles. Cut a 10" (25.4cm) from the pieced fabric. Cut a 5" (12.7cm) circle from white fabric.

4. Make the FFH. Fold the FFH base and topper pieces as usual according to the directions on page 11.

Finished six-piece FFH.

Wrong side of the sewn triangles.   Right side of the sewn triangles.

VARIATIONS

With so many different options for toppers and bases, you have endless possibilities for mixing pieced bases and toppers. Have fun experimenting.

Six-piece three-color FFH with six-piece three-color rotated topper.

Back side of six-piece fussy-cut FFH (stack and whack style).

Front side of six-piece fussy cut (stack and whack style).

Templates

This section of the book contains the circle and hexagon templates needed for the projects plus additional sizes for your own designs. Copy them onto paper or make photocopies and use them to cut out your fabric and batting.

Circle Templates

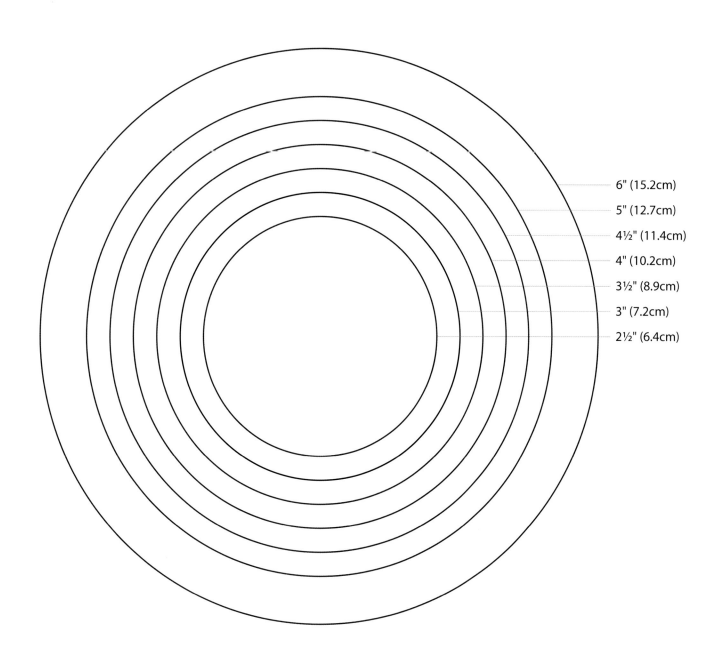

6" (15.2cm)

5" (12.7cm)

4½" (11.4cm)

4" (10.2cm)

3½" (8.9cm)

3" (7.2cm)

2½" (6.4cm)

OVERSIZE TEMPLATES

These templates do not fit on a single page and are printed across two pages for the quarter-circle. Trace both pages and join at the dotted line for a full-size template.

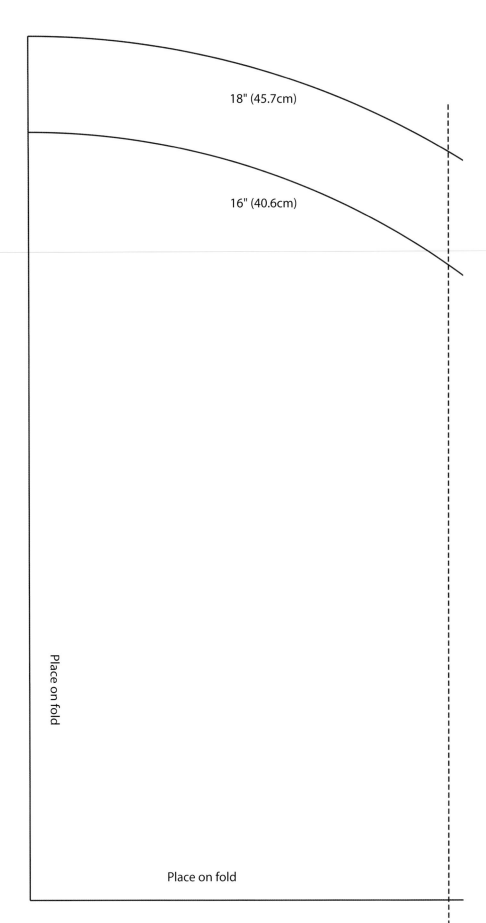

18" (45.7cm)

16" (40.6cm)

Place on fold

Place on fold

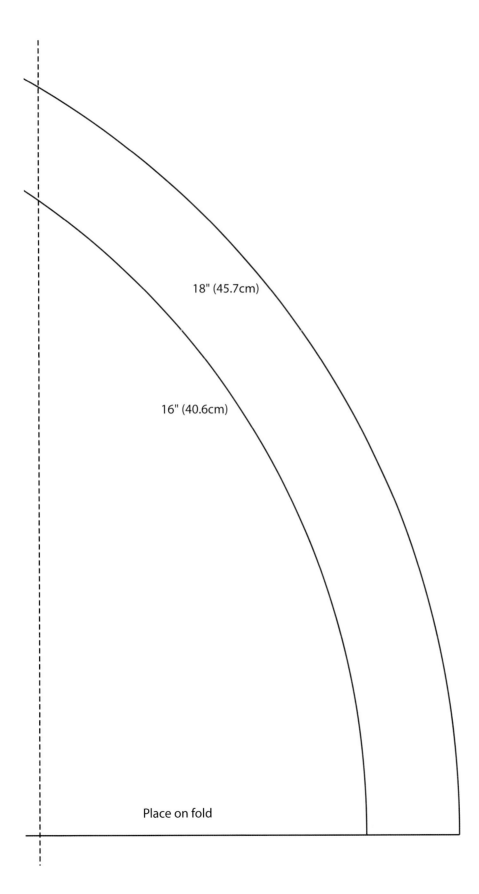

18" (45.7cm)

16" (40.6cm)

Place on fold

Fold your fabric into quarters and align these templates with the edges along the folds, as indicated.

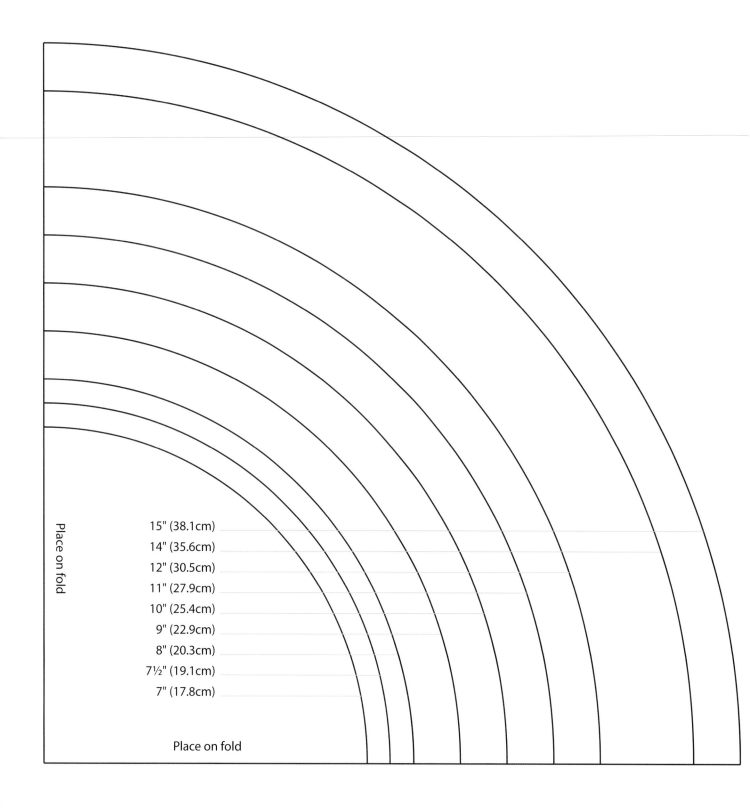

Place on fold

15" (38.1cm)
14" (35.6cm)
12" (30.5cm)
11" (27.9cm)
10" (25.4cm)
9" (22.9cm)
8" (20.3cm)
7½" (19.1cm)
7" (17.8cm)

Place on fold

Hexagon Templates

Hexagon templates are provided for all the sizes required in the book plus additional sizes for your own designs.

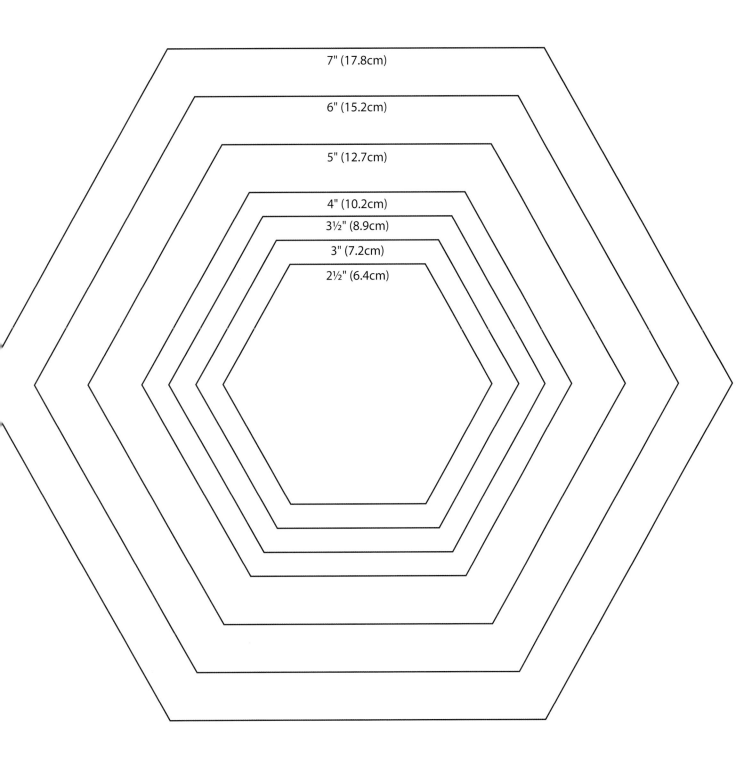

7" (17.8cm)

6" (15.2cm)

5" (12.7cm)

4" (10.2cm)

3½" (8.9cm)

3" (7.2cm)

2½" (6.4cm)

OVERSIZE TEMPLATES

These templates do not fit on a single page, so only one half is shown. Copy the template twice, and join at the dotted line for a full-size template.

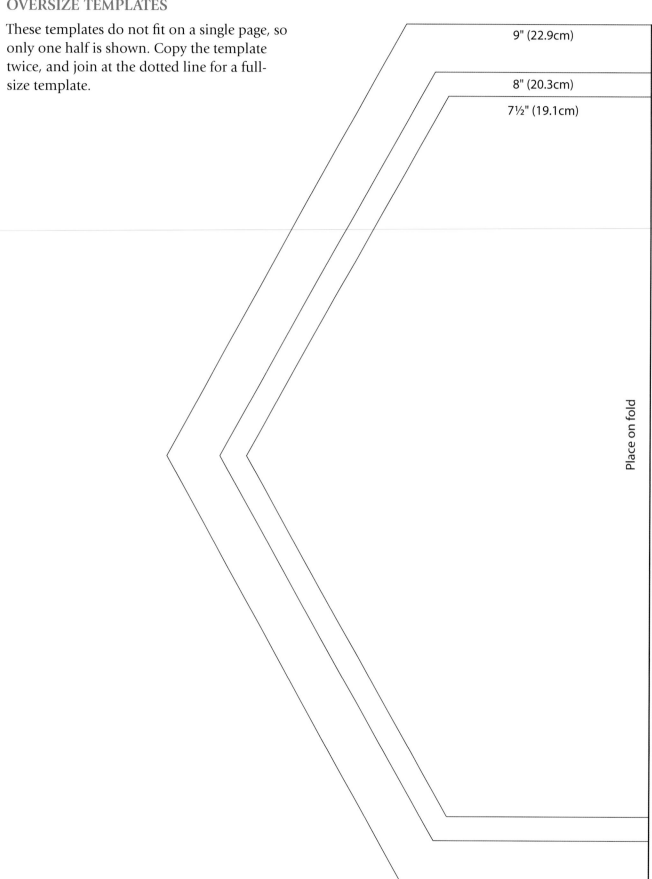

9" (22.9cm)

8" (20.3cm)

7½" (19.1cm)

Place on fold

Design Resources

Once you fall in love with FFHs, you may want to move beyond the projects in this book. To help you make and design your own FFH quilts, I've provided a number of resources to help you determine fabric requirements, layouts, and more.

Determining Fabric and Batting Amounts

It may be confusing to think about how much fabric is needed because FFHs use circles. The main thing to remember is that a 10" (25.4cm) circle can be cut from a 10" (25.4cm) square, a 5" (12.7cm) circle from a 5" (12.7cm) square, and so forth. So, instead of worrying about circles, think in terms of squares and calculate accordingly. Occasionally you can sneak a few extra circles between other circles, but for practical purposes, stick with thinking about squares.

FABRIC

For this book, the most commonly used circles are 10" (25.4cm) circles and 5" (12.7cm) circles. A 10" (25.4cm) x WOF strip yields four 10" (25.4cm) circles, and a 5" (12.7cm) x WOF strip yields eight 5" (12.7cm) circles. For all projects in this book, assume WOF = 42" (1.7m).

CIRCLES PER STRIP		
Circle size (inches)	Circle size (cm)	# per WOF
2½"	6.4cm	16
3"	7.2cm	14
3½"	8.9cm	12
4"	10.2cm	10
4½"	11.4cm	9
5"	12.7cm	8
6"	15.2cm	7
7"	17.8cm	6
7½"	19.1cm	5
8"	20.3cm	5
9"	22.9cm	4
10"	25.4cm	4
12"	30.5cm	3
14"	35.6cm	3
15"	38.1cm	2
16"	40.6cm	2
18"	45.7cm	2

The table shows the number of circles that can be cut from a 42" (1.1m) WOF strip for the circle sizes used in this book.

BATTING

The hexagons templates are measured from straight edge to straight edge (referred to as the height of the hexagon); this differs from how hexagons are typically measured (from point to point).

The hexagon template for batting is half the size as the base hexie circle.

Because batting is bulkier, does not lie as flat as fabric, and is not cut into rectangles or squares, it is more difficult to cut than fabric. I added ¾" (1.9cm) to both the height and width of the hexagon as allowance for cutting the batting strips. The batting pieces can be thought of as rectangles for purposes of determining your batting needs. To cut hexagons from strips, add ¾" (1.9cm) to the height of the hexagon (measured from straight edge to straight edge): that will be the width of your strip.

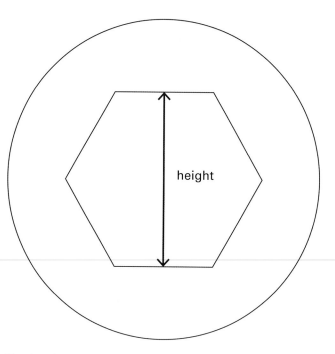

The batting hexagon is half the size of the base circle.

HEXAGONS PER STRIP			
Height of hexagon	Width of 90" (2.3m) batting strip	Number of hexagons per batting strip	Rectangle size needed for hexagon
2½" (6.4cm)	3¾" (9.5cm)	27	3¾" x 3¼" (9.5 x 8.3cm)
3" (7.6m)	4¼" (10.8cm)	24	4¼" x 3¾" (10.8 x 9.5cm)
3½" (8.9cm)	5" (12.7cm)	21	5" x 4¼" (12.7 x 10.8cm)
4" (10.2cm)	5½" (14cm)	18	5½" x 4¾" (14 x 12.1cm)
4½" (11.4cm)	6" (15.2cm)	17	6" x 5¼" (15.2 x 13.3cm)
5" (12.7cm)	6½" (16.5cm)	15	6½" x 5¾" (16.5 x 14.6cm)
6" (15.2cm)	8" (20.3cm)	13	8" x 6¾" (20.3 x 17.1cm)
7" (17.8cm)	9" (22.9cm)	11	9" x 7¾" (22.9 x 19.7cm)
7½" (19.1cm)	9½" (24.1cm)	10	9½" x 8¼" (24.1 x 21cm)
8" (20.3cm)	10" (25.4cm)	10	10" x 8¾" (25.4 x 22.2cm)
9" (22.9cm)	11¼" (28.6cm)	9	11¼" x 9¾" (28.6 x 24.8cm)

These calculations are based on 90" (2.3m) wide batting.

Suggested Quilt Dimensions

All row by column suggestions and measures are based on the use of 10" (25.4cm) circles for the FFH bases. These suggestions are a starting place for planning projects. Sometimes you need more or fewer rows or columns to accommodate a particular design.

BABY QUILTS

Quilts I designate as baby quilts are not related to the crib mattress size.*

Suggested sizes:
* 9 columns x 9 FFHs per column (81 FFHs), about 40" x 45" (1 x 1.1m)
* 10 columns x 10 FFHs per column (100 FFHs), about 44" x 50" (1.12 x 1.3m)
* 11 columns x 10 FFHs per column (110 FFHs), about 49" x 50" (1.2 x 1.3m)
* 11 columns x 11 FFHs per column (121 FFHs), about 49" x 55" (1.2 x 1.4m)

LAP QUILTS

Lap quilts do not have a specific size. They are meant to be used on a couch or chair to provide some comfort. They are understood to be larger than baby or toddler quilts but smaller than bed quilts.

Suggested sizes:
* 11 columns x 12 FFHs per column (132 FFHs), about 49" x 60" (1.2 x 1.5m)
* 13 columns x 13 FFHs per column (169 FFHs), about 55" x 65" (1.4 x 1.7m)

TWIN QUILTS

Twin quilts accommodate a standard mattress size of 39" x 75" (96.5 x 190.5cm).

Suggested sizes:
* 15 columns with 16 FFHs per column (240 FFHs), about 66" x 80" (1.7 x 2m)
* 15 columns with 17 hexagons per column (255 FFHs), about 66" x 85" (1.7 x 2.2m)
* 15 columns with 18 hexagons per column (270 FFHs), about 66" x 90" (1.7 x 2.3m)

QUEEN QUILTS

These sizes will work for a standard mattress size of 60" x 80" (1.5 x 2m).

Suggested sizes:
* 19 columns x 19 FFHs per column (361 FFHs), about 91" x 95" (2.3 x 2.4m)
* 19 columns x 20 FFHs per column (380 FFHs), about 91" x 100" (2.3 x 2.5m)
* 19 columns x 21 FFHs per column (399 FFHs), about 91" x 105" (2.3 x 2.7m)

KING QUILTS

King quilts are intended for a standard mattress size of 76" x 80" (1.9 x 2m)

Suggested sizes are:
* 23 columns x 20 FFHs per column (460 FFHs), about 101" x 100" (2.6 x 2.5m)
* 23 columns x 21 FFHs per column (483 FFHs), about 101" x 105" (2.6 x 2.7m)
* 23 columns x 22 FFHs per column (506 FFHs); about 101" x 110" (2.6 x 2.8m)

*According to the US Consumer Products and Safety Commission, it is best for babies to sleep bare, that is, with nothing in their cribs. Use a quilt only when the baby is supervised (e.g., when wrapped up in the quilt while someone is holding the baby).

Fast-Fold Hexie Design Sheet

Use this sheet to help you plan out your next quilt and make as many copies as you need. It has nineteen columns with twenty FFHs in each column.

About the Author

Mary M. Hogan is a quilter, designer, author of *String Quilt Style, Classic to Contemporary String Quilts*, and *Fast-Fold Hexies*, and former university professor who teaches at The Quilting Season in Saline, MI (www.thequiltingseason.org). She's been teaching the Fast-Fold Hexie method since 2011, and loves to push the boundaries of quilting, constantly asking "What would happen if I tried . . . ?" A passionate teacher, Mary encourages her students to bend the rules and trust their own judgment.

To see more of her work and her schedule of workshops, classes, and other events, visit her website (www.marymhogan.com).

Index